T0304094

ROUTLEDGE LIBRARY EDITIONS:
TAXATION

Volume 3

THE IMPACT OF TAX LEGISLATION ON CORPORATE INCOME SECURITY PLANNING FOR RETIREES

THE IMPACT OF TAX LEGISLATION ON CORPORATE INCOME SECURITY PLANNING FOR RETIREES

RUTH YLVISAKER WINGER

LONDON AND NEW YORK

First published in 1991 by Garland Publishing

This edition first published in 2019
by Routledge
2 Park Square, Milton Park, Abingdon, Oxon OX14 4RN

and by Routledge
711 Third Avenue, New York, NY 10017

Routledge is an imprint of the Taylor & Francis Group, an informa business

© 1991 Ruth Ylisaker Winger

British Library Cataloguing in Publication Data
A catalogue record for this book is available from the British Library

ISBN: 978-1-138-56291-2 (Set)
ISBN: 978-0-429-48988-4 (Set) (ebk)
ISBN: 978-1-138-59127-1 (Volume 3) (hbk)
ISBN: 978-0-429-49051-4 (Volume 3) (ebk)

Publisher's Note
The publisher has gone to great lengths to ensure the quality of this reprint but points out that some imperfections in the original copies may be apparent.

Disclaimer
The publisher has made every effort to trace copyright holders and would welcome correspondence from those they have been unable to trace.

THE IMPACT OF TAX LEGISLATION ON CORPORATE INCOME SECURITY PLANNING FOR RETIREES

Ruth Ylvisaker Winger

GARLAND PUBLISHING
New York & London
1991

Library of Congress Cataloging-in-Publication Data

Winger, Ruth Ylvisaker.
    The impact of tax legislation on corporate income security planning for retirees /
by Ruth Ylvisaker Winger
        p.   cm. — (Garland studies on the elderly in America)
    Includes bibliographical references.
    ISBN 0-8153-0507-9
    1. Pension trusts—United States. 2. Pension trusts—Law and legislation—United
    States. 3. Corporations—Taxation—Law and legislation—United States. 4. Compensation
    management—United States.
    I. Title. II. Series.
    HD7105.45.U6W56 1991
    658.3'253—dc20
                                                                                91-37712
                                                                                CIP

Printed on acid-free 250-year-life paper

MANUFACTURED IN THE UNITED STATES OF AMERICA

TABLE OF CONTENTS

LIST OF TABLES

ACKNOWLEDGEMENTS

The manifest purpose of this dissertation was the discovery of changing patterns of income distribution in the welfare state. This was possible because busy compensation executives in the private sector were interested in the question, and willing to contribute their time and expertise to the study. The latent, personal and more lasting purpose was to develop a dynamic sense of scholarship that could begin serving the social work profession.

When I was an undergraduate student, Thomas Rocco played a critical role in this process by illuminating for me the intimate relationship of philosophy to the applied sciences. As a graduate student, Anne Minahan's commitment to a cosmological view of social work developed my understanding of the interdependence of public policy, administrative practices, services to people and social problems. Discussions with Minahan about the tax expense system as a source of funding for social purposes turned what had been an interesting discovery during a social work field experience, into a professional challenge and a commitment of scholarly inquiry.

The transformation of the "advanced generalist practitioner" into that of "beginning scholar" was the challenging task of George Hoshino. His scholarship and wealth of knowledge, high academic standards and a never-flagging and keen interest in new knowledge,

xiii

added inspiration to the demands of scholarship. This, combined with his respect for different ways of knowing, gave me confidence in his guidance and sense of inquiry, an eagerness to learn and the desire to emulate.

During the grueling process of learning and writing, my daughters assumed the role of "mother" and kept the family traditions from falling into neglect. My son helped make the "student" role fun by treating me as a peer and acting as my advisor. My close friends continually challenged my philosophy of welfare and human services and critiqued my work. My brother John and his wife were unconditional sources of emotional and practical support. During the final desperate months, Audrey and Tony Buhl advised, fed and soothed me. Without the cheers and the commiserations of these very special people I could not have succeeded.

CHAPTER I

INTRODUCTION

Income security in old age is a topic which, by its very nature, is of universal interest. The American welfare state has become synonymous with "Social Security" to most Americans. To working citizens this means a right to collect on the social insurance they have supported through payroll taxes as an employee. Most working Americans also know that if they hope to maintain a semblance of their pre-retirement standard of living, income from social insurance will need to be supplemented. The common means of supplementing retirement income is either through personal savings and investments, or through an employer-sponsored retirement income plan, and preferably through both.

This study explored the complexities of the relationship between acts of Congress and nine major Midwest corporations in the Minneapolis-St. Paul area, regarding employer-sponsored retirement plans. Compensation executives served as the informants/respondents in a multiple-embedded case study of corporate "qualified" plans for the income protection of their retirees. The study was designed to discover if and why corporate decision makers respond to the Congress' tax incentives or the disincentives that affect the design of corporate income security plans for retirees.

1

The Social Security Act

Income protection for the aged was established as a national goal with the passage of the Social Security Act in 1935. The Social Security Act is the centerpiece of the nation's income protection for the aged. The Social Security Act mandated universal social insurance for the employed. Social insurance offers financial support for retirees, the temporarily unemployed, the disabled, and survivors. Since its enactment, amendments have expanded public programs. Social Security now includes most employed people and covers other situations of financial need, such as the permanently and totally disabled, as well as in kind supports, medical and social servies to aged, disabled low-income groups, and families with children.

Supplemental Security Income, enacted in 1972 and effective in 1974, plays a major role in the nation's income protection scheme as a guaranteed income below which the income of the elderly, blind, and the disabled cannot fall. The elderly and the disabled then, who have inadequate insurance benefits or no benefits at all, are thus protected from abject poverty (Munnell, 1978).

Despite this expansion of provisions offered by the welfare state, private provisions play a fundamental role in the nation's plan for income protection in old age. But when employers respond neither to the Congress's tax incentives nor to the employees' need to maintain a pre-retirement standard of living, the responsibility for the maintenance of an adequate standard of living in retirement lies solely with the employee and the welfare state.

The financing of retirement plans for the growing population of older Americans has been called the most important issue of the decade facing the welfare state (Underwood, 1984). Until relatively recently, the man or woman who lived beyond forty was seen as a survivor, and the one who lived beyond fifty a rare exception. The survival of the majority of the population past their working years into old age has no historical precedent and is considered one of the most profound structural changes of the modern era (Drucker, 1976).

By 1975 "retirement" had become America's newest social institution. The nation's senior citizens had quadrupled in number since the passage of the Social Security Act. Meanwhile the privately controlled pension trust funds had become the nation's largest pools of wealth and generally had been accepted as an effective mechanism for guaranteeing retirement (Drucker, 1976; McGill, 1984).

The importance of socio-economic status to individual and family social adjustment has been well documented in the literature (Eitzen, 1985). The literature also documents that income for social insurance must be supplemented if a worker's standard of living is to be maintained in retirement.

Despite the dramatic growth of private pensions over the last two decades, the data on pensions in the United States show that almost half of all employees over age forty-five will have no income security benefits other than Social Security. In addition, these employees are disproportionately represented in the lower-income levels. This represents double jeopardy, since social insurance benefits are based on the history of work-related income (Andrews, 1985; Rein, 1977).

Clearly, the protection of income in retirement is a social issue that would benefit from the interest and research of the social policy professional as well as the occupational social worker. The wisdom of understanding the social policies developed in the private sector in concert with the nation's public social policies is supported by the brief review of "social purpose" acts of Congress that follows.

Legislative History of Employee
Income Security Plans

A history of the acts of Congress that support the development of private pension plans shows an effect which first only enticed employers to participate. Later, legislation regulated the adminis- tration of those plans. Finally, between 1975 and 1985, Congress standardized the rules governing plan participation, the eligibility for benefits and the funding of employer-controlled pensions funds (see Appendix A for legislative history).

It took from 1921, when Congress first passed legislation to encourage pensions in the private sector, to 1974 and passage of the Employee Retirement Income Security Act (ERISA), to guarantee the employee's entitlement to the employer's promise of retirement benefits. With the passage of this precedent-shattering act, Congress declared that the retiree was entitled by law, under certain condi- tions, to the vested financial benefits of tax qualified retirement plans sponsored by the employer. ERISA thus entitled retirees to a lien on corporate assets if defined benefit plans were terminated by the sponsoring organization.

ERISA provided a precise definition of "qualified retirement income plans," that is, those plans eligible for preferential tax treatment or, in other words, social purpose dollars. According to P.L. 93-406 a "qualified plan" is

> . . . Any plan, fund, or program established or maintained by an employer or by an employee organization, or by both, that (a) provides retirement income to employees, or (b) results in a deferral of covered employment or beyond, regardless of the method of calculating the contributions made by the plan, the method of calculating the benefits under the plan or the method of distributing benefits from the plan.

There are important tax contingencies for both the sponsor and the beneficiary of a qualified retirement income plan which are spelled out in ERISA. A qualified plan entitles the employer to an immediate tax deduction on a future promise, and the employee to an income tax deferral until such time that the benefit is received as income.

As though to make up for lost time, by 1985 Congress had passed another five pieces of legislation to define six more employee entitlements to the qualified retirement benefits sponsored by the private sector. The next decade saw Congress systematically shape the retirement plans offered by employers to more closely reflect the egalitarian ideals of the welfare state.

The Revenue Act of 1978 set a precedent when Congress entitled the employee to tax-free savings through payroll deductions. The 1981

Economic Recovery Tax Act (ERTA) entitled employees to a corporate
vote if they participated in an Employee Stock Option Plan. (Pine and
Wright, 1982). In addition, ERTA made tax-supported incentives to
save money universally available through Individual Retirement
Accounts (IRAs) (Ludwig and Curtis, 1981).

In 1982 the Tax Equity and Fiscal Responsibility Act (TEFRA)
introduced the concept of adequacy to employer-sponsored income
protection plans. TEFRA also mitigated the corporate financial
advantage of integrating private benefits with Social Security
benefits (Carter, 1983).

In 1984 Congress passed the Deficit Reducation Act (DEFRA)
which disallowed the overfunding of "funded welfare trusts." DEFRA
also imposed an excise tax on employers who maintain trusts expressly
to provide benefits such as medical and life insurance for key
employees. DEFRA also allowed vested employees to place a lien on
corporate assets, if pension plans were terminated. DEFRA again
lowered the level at which private pensions could be integrated with
social insurance and established a maximum age at which the distribution of benefits must begin.

That same year Congress passed the Retirement Equity Act (REA)
and statutorily recognized marriage as an economic partnership. This
legislation successfully "breaches" the male "citadel" of the corporation by introducing the concept of androgeny to the workforce. With
this legislation Congress infers that the concepts of mutuality of
financial support and reciprocity of benefits are generic to the

marriage partnership. Following REA an employee's spouse, of either sex, became entitled to survivor benefits and divorce settlements that attached an employee's qualified pension plan. In addition, women became entitled to special vesting schedules in recognition of their unique childbearing/career patterns (Koski and Schneider, 1985).

The corporations have not accepted the changes of this decade without complaint. However, there is a commitment among the corporate decision makers who participated in this study to the income security of their employees. The employers see qualified retirement plans as a cost-efficient means for rewarding employee service, especially the services of key employees. They also expressed civic pride in the image portrayed by the corporation as one that is concerned for, and protects, the economic welfare of its retirees.

The growth of employer-sponsored 401(k) savings plans is testimony to the power of tax incentives to shape corporate retirement income plans. Congress has also demonstrated the ability to shape the psychology of the nation's employees. Since the Revenue Act of 1978 which introduced the popular 401(k) savings plan and the passage of ERTA in 1981 and the liberalized participation in Individualized Retirement Accounts, there has been a dramatic growth in savings within the participating corporations (Spector, 1984; Sweeney, 1984).

Again demonstrating the power of the tax acts, the passage of DEFRA led corporate compensation managers to focus on adapting the 401(k) savings plans to serve their retirement income security plans. Corporate compensation managers see the 401(k) both as an attractive cost efficient savings mechanism and an employee benefit, and also as a popular perquisite for key employees.

The move to limit the untaxed assets of "welfare trusts" has led these corporate decision makers to question Congress' continued support of the pension trust funds. The pension trusts serve to finance the greatest share of the income retirement plans offered by these corporations. The corporate decision makers suggest that the choice between corporate support for the traditional defined benefit plans financed by the pension trusts, or defined contribution plans which are pay-as-you-go plans, will be based on which is doing better financially, the corporation or the pension trust fund. The former represents a corporate promise for the future, and the latter represents opportunity in the present.

Legislation during this decade appears to be undermining the loyalty of these executives to the highly regulated qualified defined benefit plans. The informants were showing an increased interest in the less regulated defined contribution and savings plans for retirement. The rationale for Congress' action is assumed to be twofold by this investigator. First, the nation's expressed need for capital formation. This need can be satisfied both by creating a psychology of saving and by breaking down the financial control of the pension trust funds to created a broader tax base. Second, Congress has become aware of the significant changes that have taken place in the demographics of the nation's workforce during the last two decades. These changes have created an incongruence between the traditional goals of

qualified pension plans and the self-interest of the contemporary
employee (U.S. Congress, House, Select Committee on Aging, Future of
Retirement Programs, 1987).

1975 to 1985 can be called Congress' Decade of the Employee.
The employee entitlements established by ERISA and subsequent legislation have significant implications for the income security of
retirees of the modern corporation. Congress has established the
statutory right of plan participants to vested benefits, to government
subsidized personal savings accounts, and to employee ownership of
business for participants in Employee Stock Option Plans (ESOPs).
Further, Congress introduced a measure of need based on adequacy,
rather than the traditional measure which includes status and merit,
to the private sector. Not satisfied, Congress also established the
statutory entitlement of the pre and post retiree to a lien on corporate assets. Following DEFRA, the first obligation of the failed
corporation (even before federal taxes!) is to satisfy their pension
plan obligations in accordance with federal regulations. DEFRA also
applies to corporations that terminate their pension plans for any
reason.

In this same decade it is significant that Congress recogn-
nized marriage as an economic partnership and established by statute
the entitlement of spouses and divorcess to corporate retirement and
death benefits. Congress also now recognizes the unique differences
in the employment patterns of women, while at the same time

establishing equal treatment of the sexes in the distribution of retirement benefits.

In this "Decade of the Employee," Congress has changed the structure of "contingent welfare." Employee benefits are now no longer contingent only on the relationship of the employee to the employer. Now publically supported employer benefits for the protection of income in retirement are also contingent on the relationship of the employer to Congress. Further, the accountability of the employer for attention to the rights of benefit plan participants is subject to public oversight by the Internal Revenue Service (IRS). This effectively establishes a form of "quality compliance," a concept familiar to public service professionals.

These changes, however, come with a price tag for the employee. If defined contribution plans become the primary corporate vehicle for the protection of post-work income this will represent a change in the locus of responsibility. Defined contribution plans place the financial responsibility for the future with the employee. Conversely, the defined benefit plans place the responsibility for income protection with the employer. Plan participants need to be aware that a change to defined contribution plans places the financial risks with the employee, and the Congress offers no protections to the destitute retiree other than public programs. With defined benefit plans the financial risks of the unknowns in the future are born by the employer, plus the employee enjoys the added financial protection of the Pension Benefit Guarantee Corporation when the sponsor fails to meet the promised obligation.

An interesting compromise to the above dilemma, which tolerates some of Congress' pension plan disincentives, is represented by the Toro Corporation's design for the income security of their support staff. This "floor plan" is based on the company-wide defined contribution plan but, unlike conventional designs, this plan is backed up by a defined benefit plan. The pension plan comes into play if the employee's defined contribution benefits fail to meet a pre-determined minimum based on pre-retirement income. In this way the risks of the future are shared by the employee and the employer. This model for the protection of employees in the lower earning bracket emulates the model developed by the walfare state. In the welfare model, federal Supplemental Security Income, a guaranteed minimum income for the aged, blind and disabled, comes into play as a status right for those elderly whose Social Security benefits fail to meet a predetermined minimum.

The Public-Private Hybrid of the American Welfare State

Despite the voluntary nature of privately sponsored pension plans, welfare policy is explicit in identifying private pensions as a part of the nation's scheme for income protection of the aged. Private income security plans are seen as one leg of the national three-legged stool for income protection in old age. Congress expects that private pensions will supplement Social Security benefits and individual savings to meet the economic needs of

12

retirement. The yardstick accepted as adequate for income protection
in retirement is a sixty to seventy percent replacement of pre-
retirement income through Social Security, corporate pensions and
personal savings.

Besides offering employers tax incentives to encourage collaboration with the state in achieving income protection for retirees,
Congress has allowed employers to integrate private benefits with the
expected Social Security benefits (Schultz and Leavitt, 1983). The
integration of private plans with Social Security is a technical
procedure which uses the projected Social Security pension as a base
from which to establish the private pension benefit. This serves to
unify the two systems to achieve an income formula that is considered
adequate protection in retirement. From the perspective of Congress,
integration is a technique which avoids the use of public funds to
over-pension the retiree. From the perspective of the employer, it is
a technique which guards against the lower-paid employee earning more
during retirement than while working. Integration offers the employer
the most dollar efficient means of funding income security plans.
This publicly sanctioned method of establishing the retirement benefit
also effectively ties the lower-paid employee to a lower-paid
retirement check.

The integration of Social Security and private pensions
creates an "interlocking" public and private partnership in a "hybrid"
approach to a single income replacement goal for retirees (Root, 1982).

Congress has encouraged integration in recognition of the employer's contribution to Social Security (Schultz and Leavitt, 1983).

The social importance of corporate pensions to the welfare state is reflected in the income level of the ERISA plan beneficiaries. In 1983, 70 percent of these retirees had earned less than $25,000 annually. This was at a cost of $87.1 billion to the private sector. In economic terms the corporate pension system also has a significant impact on the nation. The financial assets tied up in the nation's pension trust funds in 1985 totalled 863 billion dollars. Clearly, corporate pensions are big business, and a business that protects the retirement income of many "ordinary" people (Andrews, 1985; Beam and McFadden, 1985; Kotlikoff and Smith, 1983).

Current Status of Pension Plans

From a financial standpoint, pensions are big business, but a business that is changing. The initiation of new pensions into the private sector decreased by 50 percent following the passage of ERISA. Before 1974, the number of plans was increasing at the rate of 15 percent per year, but by 1985 the rate of increase had slowed to 7 percent (Andrews, 1985). This concerns Congress at a time when Social Security assets, the welfare state's centerpiece for the income protection of retired citizens, are threatened. The problem is compounded by the knowledge that the older population is expected to reach 40.3 million by 2020 and will enjoy an extended retirement of seventeen years in contrast to the average duration of retirement in

1935 of 12.8 years (U.S. Congress, House, Committee on Economic Development, Reforming Retirement Policies, 1981; U.S. Congress, House, Special Committee on Aging, "Tenth Anniversary of the Employee Retirement Act," 1984).

CHAPTER II

BACKGROUND OF THE STUDY

The Titmuss Model for Policy Analysis

The theoretical background of this investigation is based on
the work of Richard Titmuss, the British philosopher-economist and
critic of the welfare state (Titmuss, 1963). Titmuss examined the
relationship of the rapidly developing national tax system in an
industrialized economy to the social policies of the infant welfare
state. His observations led to the identification of what he referred
to as the "Iceberg Phenomenon of Social Welfare" and a model for the
analyses of this phenomenon.

The Iceberg Phenomenon of
Social Welfare

Titmuss (1968) used the analogy of the iceberg to emphasize
the unrecognized benefits which accrue to citizens of the welfare
state through tax policies which he saw becoming an "alternative to
legislated social policy" (p. 190). He contended that the consideration of social policy in isolation from economic policy was incomplete since "each factor contributing to economic change also
contributes to social change" (p. 191). Titmuss called for a broader
definition of social welfare than is generally held by social
scientists, a definition of "welfare" that includes tax-related
fiscal and occupational benefits within the rubric of social welfare.

15

To appreciate the Titmuss perspective of welfare, it is
necessary to have a clear picture of the dual structure of the
nation's tax system. For the purpose of this study the investigator
defines all the dollars collected through the national tax system as
the "national purse." This national purse includes (a) those taxes
that are collected by the Internal Revenue Service for the government,
and (b) those taxes imposed by the government but which, for one
reason or another, are not collected.

The national tax aggregate that results from this dual
approach can be compared with the wealth of a landlord who collects
rent monthly from certain tenants. The landlord effectively increases
his "purse" as well as the social and economic alternatives that are
available to him in the market. That same landlord, for some reason,
may choose to forego the rent for certain tenants. The effect of this
decision is to reduce the disposable income, or "the purse", of the
landlord and thus the available social and economic choices. However,
the landlord then increases the disposable income and the number of
social and economic choices available to the tenant. In both cases
the landlord's net income, that is, the purse, has changed and the
"household budget" is adjusted accordingly.

The first case is analagous to the national system of tax
appropriation which increases the size of the national purse, and the
second to the national system of tax expenditures which decrease the
size of the national purse. Patterns of income distribution change in
significant ways depending on the landlord's decision. Titmuss

pointed out that the relationship of the tax system to social welfare also changes in several ways depending on the choice of legislatures to appropriate tax dollars or use the "expense" method to meet the obligations of the welfare state.

At the broadest level, tax appropriation is a matter of public and statutory policy established by an act of Congress, and is subject to public oversight. Tax expenses, on the other hand, are a result of Congressional discretion, which are also legislated and defined by the rules and standards of the IRS. Using the analogy of the landlord, the patterns of economic and social distribution practiced by the nation-landlord are affected by the decision to collect or not to collect taxes (or rent). Second, the new dollar aggregate, which might be bigger or smaller, depending on the case in question, will define the limits within which the nation's (or landlord's) alternatives exist and choices can be made. Third, the locus of the control of social purpose dollars changes, depending on the tax method. The dollar amount remains the same, but the decision makers in control of redistribution change from the public sector decision makers to private sector decision makers.

Recognizing the interdependence and the complexity of economic and social issues of the welfare state, Titmuss urged the adoption of a wider, more appropriate frame of reference for the definition of welfare. Using the iceberg analogy, the visible "tip of the iceberg" represents programs such as Aid to Families with Dependent Children (AFDC) and is perceived by the public to be "welfare". Titmuss

contended, however, that the economic and social resources distributed
to the citizens of the welfare state are represented by the entire
iceberg. For instance, fiscal welfare allows exemptions and deductions
on individual income tax returns for dependent children and can be seen
as "aid to dependent children." Occupational welfare includes such
benefits as the subsidization of the costs incurred in the adoption of
children by employees and the provision of day care services. These
benefits can also be seen as "aid to families with dependent children."
These forms of social welfare fall "under the water line" of the
welfare iceberg and are hidden from the public's perception and
consciousness.

This broader definition of welfare clarifies for the critic
and the analyst the limitations of examining and analyzing only the
policies and programs of the welfare state that are "clearly visible,
direct and immediately measurable" (p. 192), that is, the tip of the
iceberg.

The Titmuss Model for Social
Policy Analysis

In his seminal article, "The Social Division of Welfare,"
Titmuss (1963) equates the tip of the iceberg with those "social
welfare" functions that (a) are represented by services and institutions recognized by the public to have clearly been developed for the
"poor and the unlucky" (p. 52), (b) are financed through Congressional
appropriations, and (c) are subjected to regular public oversight, and
private criticism.

19

The submerged portion of the iceberg hides from public view, consciousness and oversight two parallel systems, fiscal and occupational welfare, which have developed incrementally over time to meet the needs of citizens in highly organized and complex societies. Titmuss found that fiscal and occupational benefits were a response to the dependency needs of the citizens of an industrialized, highly specialized and complex society. By definition then, these benefits authorized by Congress, can be considered welfare. The consequence of the limited public acknowledgement of fiscal and occupational benefits as social welfare has been that the systems are "appraised, criticized or applauded as abstracted, independent entities, and for this reason, as presently organized, they are simultaneously enlarging and consolidating the area of social inequality" (pp. 53, 55).

Titmuss proposed the fiscal-occupational-social model for social policy analyses to demonstrate the full scope of the nation's social welfare activity. The use of this model was expected to more accurately reflect the redistribution of benefits in the modern welfare state.

Fiscal welfare is made up of those benefits and advantages which are available through the individual personal tax system such as exemptions for the number of dependents, child-care credits, home mortgage interest deductions or head of household credits. They represent support from states of social dependency endemic to a highly developed and specialized industrial society. Titmuss (1963,

1974) found fiscal welfare beneficial, redistributive and concerned with both economic and non-economic objectives.

Occupational welfare also plays a significant role in the redistributive function of the welfare state and is also "submerged" from the public's consciousness as a benefit of the welfare state. Benefits and services include pensions for employees, insurance policies, survivors' benefits, health plans, paid sick leave, severance pay, moving expenses, education and training opportunities as well as in-kind benefits such as meals and free parking. Titmuss (1963) nicknamed occupational welfare "contingent welfare" (p. 53) because in this model of redistribution individual need is contingent on employment status and merit. This is true despite the fact that the cost of benefits is highly subsidized by all citizens through the progressive tax system.

Social welfare is represented by that portion of the iceberg which is "obvious and measurable" and with which human service professionals and the public more readily identify. "Social" welfare includes direct benefits with which the public is familiar, such as income maintenance payments and services in kind, provided by both public and quasi-public organizations. Benefits might include public assistance, health services, education, housing, and more recently, the "personal social services." These "personal services" include family and children's services and services to the aged and the mentally ill. Table 1 illustrates these welfare policies.

21

TABLE 1

PUBLIC WELFARE POLICY

Kind of Welfare	Income Maintenance	Health	Housing	Education	Employment	Personal Social Services
Fiscal welfare	Tax-free transfers; tax exemptions for children, self, spouse	Deduction for health costs; health insurance	Deduction for home mortgage interest	Low-interest loans for college costs	Deduction for moving costs; training costs	Child care tax credit; dependent care tax credit; pretax dollars for medical expenses
Occupational welfare	Pensions; severance pay; paid sick leave; on-site meals	Company health plans; wellness programs	Company housing; moving costs; low-interest loans	Continuing education; scholarships for employee children; education leave	On-the-job training; retraining	Daycare; EAP(1)
Social welfare	Unemployment compensation; Social Security; AFDC(3); SSI(4); food stamps	Medicare; Medicaid; WIC(2) veterans services	Public housing	Head Start; public education	Targeted jobs program; workfare; work-study; public works	Daycare; Meals-on-Wheels; community care

SOURCE: Adapted from Hoshino, 1985.
NOTE: (1) Employee Assistance Programs, (2) Nutrition for Women, Infants and Children, (3) Aid to Families with Dependent Children, (4) Supplemental Security Income.
NOTE: This is a visual demonstration that the Titmuss theory of public policy, through legislation and tax laws, benefits particular segments of the population. It is incomplete and limited to examples.

Consequences of Social Compartmentalization

Titmuss (1963) found this propensity to define social welfare to the exclusion of fiscal and occupational welfare had compartmentalized social welfare just as the welfare society has conceptually, perceptually and professionally compartmentalized the poor. This compartmentalism has led to a failure of social policy proponents to recognize that all tax monies, either appropriated and distributed, or expensed and "forgiven", represent alternate means that are used by Congress to legislate social policy.

Titmuss was critical of fiscal welfare for its propensity to emphasize a fairness between taxpayers or, in other words, fairness between "contributors" to the coffers of the national tax system. This emphasis on fairness between taxpayers usurps the meaning of fairness in the welfare state. The concept of fairness within the context of the welfare state, according to Titmuss (pp. 53, 74), must be based on citizenship, rather than the amount of tax paid by individuals or groups of individuals. This just distribution between all citizens is based on the relationship of the citizen's need and the resources of the welfare state.

Titmuss was critical of social redistribution through occupational benefit systems for undermining both the working population's support for public programs and for the principles of equal and equitable redistribution. Titmuss found the social conscience of the employed, with occupational welfare at their disposal, to be less sensitive to those individuals victimized by a changing industrialized society. Of critical importance to the analyst is an awareness that occupationally welfare benefits are associated with the primary labor market, that is, with well-established employers where it can be expected that employees benefit from higher wages and more job security. Contrasted to this is the secondary labor market where wages are lower, jobs are less secure, benefits are few or absent, and where the employees are disproportionately represented by women and minorities.

The Future of the Welfare State

Titmuss's (1963) criticism of the growing social division of welfare does not seem to be on the use per se of fiscal and occupational channels for social redistribution. Rather, he seems critical of the failure of the public, the politicians, social policy proponents and analysts to recognize and act on the interdependence and integrative potential of fiscal, occupational and social welfare (p. 74). The consequence of excluding fiscal and occupational welfare policy from an inclusive definition of social welfare he saw as having exascerbated social inequalities and inequities.

Titmuss predicted that the maintenance of an egalitarian distribution of the tax resources would pose a significant problem for the twentieth century welfare state in America. He posited this prediction on the rapid rate at which the average income of the citizens was rising, the tradition of taxation and on the measures used to determine the distribution of social resources in the American welfare state.

Distribution of social benefits is not only based on need but also on the individual's "status", defined as "private wealth", and the individual's "merit" which is associated with labor market performance. Titmuss points out that these combined qualifications, when incomes rise, widen the gap between income classes and also result in patterns of distribution of tax resources that exacerbate inequality and inequity among citizens. In addition, citizens' resistance to supporting the tax system is strengthened. The fact that the welfare state's resources consist of the citizens' tax dollars creates a situation where the beneficiaries of the state, the citizens, see themselves as the victim of the tax system. The citizen tends to see the nation's tax obligations as an economic issue separate from that of benefits enjoyed in a welfare state. The focus is on what the citizens pays rather than on the credits, exclusions and benefits accrued. At the national level this separation of economic policy from the issue of support for the benefits of social policy considerations obfuscates the interdependence of economic and social issues from the planners and policy analysts of the welfare state. Indeed, we should note that direct appropriations by Congress are determined by the House and Senate Appropriations Committees when tax expenditures are determined by the House Ways and Means Committee and the Senate Finance Committee.

Titmuss saw that this perceptual and conceptual separation of economic and social policy, this inattention to "wholes", had created patterns of distribution in the welfare state which nourish rather than mitigate social inequality and inequity. He called for "a new approach . . . we cannot delineate the new frontiers of poverty unless we take account of the changing agents and characteristics of inequality" (p. 77).

The consequences of this failure to consider the "whole" have been to afford the welfare symbolized by the submerged portion of the iceberg the lion's share of the welfare state's resources. These resources, hidden from view of the general public's consciousness and oversight, tend to favor those citizens with better jobs and/or higher income tax brackets. Titmuss identified those citizens as coming largely from the middle class.

The Titmuss Philosophy
of the Welfare State

Although Titmuss was a prolific writer, and a thoughtful critic of the welfare state, he did not develop a theory to support his model of fiscal-occupational-social welfare. There is widespread agreement however, that models require theoretical underpinnings to provide a framework for analysis and to develop an understanding of the problem at hand (Geroch, 1978; Kettner, Daley and Nichols, 1985). In the absence of a theory of the welfare state this investigator has compiled some of the social critics' observations, principles, and philosophical positions on the modern welfare state.

These observations focus on the following topics germane to the modern welfare state. First, the structure of the welfare state which Titmuss saw as unilateral and integrative; second, the principles upon which the modern welfare state should be based, seen by the critic as altruism and justice; third, the purpose of the welfare state; fourth, the criteria for social welfare policy; fifth, the assumptions upon which Titmuss based his observations.

The act of organizing Titmuss's concepts revealed a surprising consistency with General Systems Theory (GST) developed by von Bertalanffy (1968). The relationship of the four general presuppositions of GST and the work of Titmuss will be discussed.

The Structure of the Welfare State

There are two distinguishing features of Titmuss's (1968) concept of the modern welfare state. First, Titmuss sees the distribution of welfare to citizens as a unilateral transfer from the state to the individual. This transfer he defined as an unconditional "grant" or "gift" (p. 22) which might be in the form of cash, time, energy, satisfaction, blood or even life itself. Titmuss considered this grant or gift as the hallmark of social welfare in the modern state.

The second distinguishing feature of the welfare state is "its focus on integrative systems, that is, on processes, transactions and institutions which promote an individual's sense of identity, participation and community" (Titmuss, 1971, pp. 223-224).

A major and continuing concern for Titmuss was the clarification of the distinction between social policy and economic policy. He identified the socializing values of a welfare society as altruism and justice. He saw these values as antithetical to the industrialized capitalist economy. Distribution, according to Titmuss, while unilateral and unconditional through the social welfare system, is conditional, and one of exchange in the market system.

Titmuss framed the welfare state's social policies as a direct and reactive response to the social problems that are created by a developed nation's economic policies. His insistence on their conceptual and functional separation was unflagging. This writer finds it interesting that Titmuss was able to see that conceptual compartmentalization of fiscal occupational and social welfare had led to the iceberg phenomenon of welfare, but yet required a compartmentalization of economic and social systems. This separation of economic and social policy would seem to contradict the very principle of integration that Titmuss proposes. However, if Titmuss defined the concept of unilateral distribution in the welfare state at a high level of abstraction to refer to the welfare state's unconditional regard for citizens made manifest through democratic redistribution, then the principle of a unilateral transfer has some consistency.

Principles of the Modern Welfare State

Titmuss saw the evolution of the modern welfare state as dependent on a collective philosophy of altruism and justice. According to Titmuss, when altruism is the basis for actions taken by the state to achieve social equality and equity then the propensity for altruism is promoted among citizens of the state. Through this "role modelling" by the state, altruism becomes the common value which socializes the society to the ideals of the egalitarian state.

Titmuss found that altruism has two components, intent and regard. Altruistic acts of social redistribution are based on the "intention" of the welfare state to act with "regard" for citizens.

28

"An altruistic act is recognized by the intention to act in a manner
designed with regard for the interests of other persons" (Eccles and
Robinson, 1984, p. 79). Titmuss contended that the welfare society
based on altruism will reject egoism and self-interest for a fusion of
intelligence and concern for justice.

The second principle, justice, is defined as a respect for
persons, mutuality and reciprocity between citizens and the state, and
equality in all human relations (Titmuss, 1974, pp. 23-32). Justice
as it applies to the welfare state also has two components identified
by Titmuss (1971, p. 126). The first, proportional justice, addresses
the principle of equity and the rights of recipients in social redistribution. The second component, creative justice, addresses the
right of access to resources of the welfare state.

The attainment of the ideals of a modern welfare state,
according to Titmuss (1974, pp. 132-141), are dependent on a society
that expresses compassion for one another. In his opinion, such
compassion requires both a collective philosophy of social justice and
a formal system for public accountability. For the modern welfare
state to reach its full potential Titmuss further contended that the
altruistic and just society must be characterized by creativity
coupled with tolerance.

The Purpose of the Welfare State

Titmuss found six major reasons for the existence of a welfare
state (Wilding, 1976). These are:

1. Social welfare exists to distribute and redistribute income in a range of ways and directions among all the citizens of the state (Titmuss, 1968, pp. 184-5).

2. Social welfare exists to promote social integration and social harmony while reducing the problems caused by discrimination and injustice. Social policy is meant to further the sense of community and participation, prevent alienation, and serve to integrate the members of minority groups into the larger society (Titmuss, 1968, p. 65).

3. Social welfare exists to ameliorate the social costs inherent in the complex and changing (post) industrialized society, characterized by man-made dependencies. "Our growing inability to identify and connect cause and effect in the world of social and technological change is thus one reason for the historical emergence of social welfare institutions . . ." (Titmuss, 1963).

4. Social welfare exists to promote individual and social well-being by enhancing the life of those with special needs through the provision of services.

5. Social welfare exists as society's investment in healthy and educated citizens and should not be analyzed in terms of costs of current expenditures. Social welfare expenditures can make a positive contribution to the national income as well as to national welfare.

6. Social welfare exists to provide a means for citizens to exercise the "biological need to help." Titmuss (1971) saw giving as a vital element in modern society, gaining in importance as dependency

increases. Social institutions can "facilitate the expression of man's moral sense . . . can help actualize the social and moral potentialities of all citizens" (p. 238).

The Criteria for Policies
of the Welfare State

Titmuss was quite explicit throughout his writings on his criteria for social policies of the welfare state. The broad definition of social welfare presented by Titmuss highlights the importance of social work scholars having a cohesive and integrated set of criteria for social policy analyses. Titmuss suggested the following comprehensive set of social policy criteria as appropriate for policy analyses in an egalitarian society.

1. Social policy should be deliberately egalitarian, which in practice calls for universal policies.

2. Policies should be geared to the eradication of poverty and benefits set at an "adequate" rather than subsistence level.

3. Policies for dependents should be characterized by altruism rather than market criteria so that the elderly and other dependent groups can live as much like other people as possible.

4. Policies should be responsive to changing society, to skill obsolescence, to the changing role of women, to the changing burden of dependency so that the costs of change are equitably shared.

5. Finally, social policies should offer the citizen a choice as to how and when they receive benefits and a right to participate in the discussion of terms and conditions.

The Underlying Assumptions
of the Welfare State

In "The Social Divison of Welfare," Titmuss (1963) identifies
and discusses four commonly held but false assumptions which he felt
had led to the Iceberg Phenomenon of Social Welfare. These false
assumptions are:

1. With the passage of the Social Security Act in 1935 the
welfare state had fulfilled its promise and was approaching the end
of social reform.

2. The aggregate redistributive effect and defining characteristic of the welfare state is a transfer of economic resources from
those who are rich to those who are poor.

3. It is possible to categorically define what constitutes a
social service in the welfare state.

4. Social policy is represented only by those programs which
are "visible, direct and measurable." This assumes that only the
direct provisions of cash or in kind constitute the benefits of
"welfare" and this tip of the iceberg defines the nature and function
of the welfare state.

A Restatement

It is instructive to restate these assumptions considered
false by Titmuss, in reverse, to clarify the assumptions upon which
Titmuss did in fact base his philosophy of the welfare state. By
reversing the Titmuss statements one can posit that his concepts of
the modern welfare state are based on the following assumptions:

1. The welfare state is not the "effective operation of various services" (Titmuss, 1963, p. 34) but rather a cognitive-humanist construct; that is, a complex image or idea held by a collective society, suited to an industrial age, where the welfare state is in an evolutionary state. Titmuss implies that the construct which defines the welfare state and the construct which defines redistribution, are synonymous and interchangeable; that is, the welfare state IS redistribution of the nation's resources, and redistribution of the nation's resources IS the function of a welfare state. This construct of the welfare state also implies social integration and the equal and equitable redistribution of a nation's resources. Titmuss saw redistribution in the welfare state as an expression of that society's universal wish to meet the needs of the dependent members of society, and as a reflection of the modern state's wish to survive as an integrated whole. These survival goals of a welfare state are met through changes in the patterns of distribution of the nation's economic and social resources.

2. Titmuss saw the nature of the patterns for redistribution in the welfare state as dependent on the economic and social need of the situation which created the dependency. The states of dependency that are of concern to the welfare state are not only those that result from socio-economic poverty, but natural dependencies such as childhood and old age, as well as conditions of physical and psychological ill-health. In addition to these traditionally accepted dependencies, Titmuss (1963) identified a host of social and cultural,

or as he said, "man-made" dependencies common to a modern industrialized society. Such dependencies are created by unemployment, under-
employment, retirement from work, delayed entry of the young into the
labor market and technological obsolescence of workers. He saw these
dependencies as structural problems of the economic system, which
could only be alleviated through structural changes in the market
system (p. 48).

    3. It is not possible in a welfare state to identify each
beneficiary of welfare, or who bears the cost of the welfare enjoyed
by the citizens. Titmuss saw that social services encompassed a
"multitude of heterogenous activities" which are designed to meet the
constantly changing needs of individual citizens. It is important to
note that Titmuss found there could be no constant principle for the
definition of social services. The only constant, according to
Titmuss, is change itself. In other words, the only constant principles of the social welfare are the constantly changing social
situations in modern society and the welfare state's changing
response to the survival of society, designed to meet the new
anticipated dependency needs.

    4. Titmuss found it necessary to broaden the public defini-
tion of welfare to include all of the welfare iceberg. He found that
the lack of public awareness of the growing social division of welfare
in the developing welfare state had served to inhibit the ultimate
democratic goal. This goal he saw as social and economic equality and
equity through the redistribution of a nation's resources. If

progress is to be made toward this ideal, he found that it would be necessary to recognize and consider all sources of redistribution. Titmuss found that only through a heightened awareness can a society avoid unintended, self-defeating consequences which inhibit the full development of the welfare state.

General Systems Theory and
the Titmuss Philosophy

Scholars have lamented the fact that Titmuss did not develop a theory of the welfare state. He did, however, express many ideas which are congruent with his contemporary, Ludwig Von Bertalanffy (1968), the "father" of General Systems Theory (GST). Bertalanffy presented General Systems Theory to the scientific community as a meta-theory that fuses the cognitive and the perceptual. He calls GST a "new natural philosophy" and defines GST as a disciplinary matrix which allows the fusion of facts with values. The advantages of this fusion of fact and value, or in other words, the objective and the subjective worlds, is analogous to the advantages of creating atomic energy through fusion over creating atomic energy through fission.

When the scientific world solved the problem of how to split the atom, there was a great deal of excitement about atomic energy as a cost efficient, infinite source of energy. This happened, too, when the "scientific method" was perfected. Atomic energy, however, comes at the price of life-threatening nuclear "waste". Similarly, the scientific method in the social sciences has come at the price of "contextual waste." Natural scientists now are struggling to solve the problems of how to fuse the atom. It is anticipated that atomic energy through fusion is indeed the infinite source of energy the world needs, and it will come without nuclear waste since the technology is based on the principles of synergy. GST proposes the fusion of the knowledge of the natural and the social sciences and promises a knowledge explosion with a minimum of wasted human potential.

It can be posited that the infant welfare state has been developed on the principles of fission. What Titmuss seems to be suggesting is a need for policy professionals and the public to adopt a conceptual-perceptual framework that recognizes the synergy created through the fusion of atoms, if the potential of the evolving welfare state is to be realized.

The Titmuss model for policy analyses addresses the advantages of a welfare state based on the principles of fusion and the disadvantages of a welfare state developed on the principles of fission. The presuppositions of GST presented by Von Bertalanffy are surprisingly congruent with the assumptions on which Titmuss based his philosophy.

General Systems Theory is based on four central presuppositions: holism, interdependence, unity and humanism. Holism addressed the phenomenon of organized complexity found in modern societies. Holism challenges the traditional atomism and mechanism of the scientific community. GST identifies wholes and their related parts as important. Like Von Bertalanffy, Titmuss (1963) did not see "that it is practicable, desirable and has any meaning in a complex society to abstract a 'social service world' from the Greater Society, and to consider the functions and effects of the part without reference to the life of the whole" (p. 39).

The second shared presupposition is that of integration. Bertalanffy identified the integration of hitherto diverse concepts and theories. He conceptualized the emerging ismorphies in scientific theories in this century as the invariances of science. Integration is characterized by equifinality which allows more than a single means for achieving a common end.

Titmuss found that it was not possible in a welfare state to identify each beneficiary of welfare, or each bearer of the cost of welfare. Titmuss found that the concept of social services encompassed a multitude of heterogeneous activity. He found these activities were designed to meet the constantly changing needs of individual citizens. He identified change as the invariance in the welfare society. Titmuss also identified the differentiated means by which the welfare state achieved its single goal of a welfare society. This is consistent with the concept of equifinality in GST.

The third of Bertalanffy's presuppositions addresses the unity in science. He found that all theories manifest analogous strands of order. He suggests that the world is governed by the same kind of fundamental laws in all its different realms, denying the traditional dualism of science and phenomenon.

Titmuss (1963) identified harmony as a common denominator among the purposes of welfare. He insisted that the welfare state and not the "effective operation of various services" (p. 34) but rather a single complex image or idea held by the collective society. He implied that the concept of the "welfare state" and "redistribution" were synonymous and indivisible.

Titmuss found that it was necessary to broaden the public definition of welfare to include all of the social welfare iceberg. He found that progress towards the welfare society could not be made unless society simultaneously recognized all forms of dependency, both man-made and natural, as well as all forms of social and economic resources. He contended that the welfare state must be based on a holistic view of society with policies which promote integration and undermine discrimination.

The fourth presupposition shared by GST and Titmuss is humanism as the responsibility of science. This assumes a need for what Von Bertalanffy calls "design theory." Titmuss might have identified his fiscal-occupational-social welfare model with design theory which fuses fact and value, and challenges the exclusive use of scientific theories based on reductionism. The philosophical position held by Titmuss that no welfare state can mature ideologically unless based on altruism and justice is consistent with GST's mandate to fuse fact and value. GST and the Titmuss philosophy call for a fusion of science and phenomenology, in the evaluation of social policy.

Given the above evidence of the congruence between GST and the writings of Titmuss, it might be useful for the social scientist seeking a theory to support the Titmuss model for social policy

38

analyses to further explore the cognitive fit between the Titmuss
philosophy of the welfare state and Von Bertalanffy's GST. It is this
writer's opinion that Titmuss was, in fact, a General System Theorist
who applied the principles expressed in GST to the empirical problems
of the emerging welfare state.

Application of the Titmuss Welfare Model
to Critical Examinations of Welfare State

Contemporary scholars have applied the Titmuss fiscal-
occupational-social welfare model to critically examine the relationship of economic and social redistribution in the American welfare
state to the nation's tax policy.

General Discussion of the Titmuss
Model in the Welfare State

Martin Rein (1977) reiterates the Titmuss call for an
egalitarian redistribution of national resources and a conceptual
synthesis of fiscal, occupational and social welfare. Like Titmuss,
Rein finds that the tax system shapes and creates national social
policy. The application of the Titmuss model for policy analyses by
Rein exposes how the three categories of welfare are played against
one another to undermine equitable distributive welfare policies.

Unlike Titmuss, Rein claims no distinction between macro-
economic policies and social policy, and does not expect analysts to
make intelligent policy choices without recognizing this phenomenon.
According to Rein, not only is social policy affecting economic

policy, but economic policy is equally decisive for framing social
policies.

Rein differs from Titmuss on significant points. He dis-
agrees that unilateral welfare policies alone can counteract economic
practices and achieve an equitable redistribution of the nation's
resources. Social welfare policy which responds to the economically
induced dependencies of an industrialized nation have been recommended by Titmuss. Rein, however, recommonds pro-active measures at
the national level that simulataneously impact both economic and
social policy, in recognition of a co-dependency.

Titmuss fully recognized the necessity of integrating social
policy with national economic policy, yet insisted on an administratively "compartmentalized" and reactive approach to social and
economic problems by the welfare state. Titmuss's commitment to a
unilateral system of redistribution which reacts to economically
induced dependencies is consistent throughout his writings. This
might be explained by the fact that basic to the welfare state as
envisioned by Titmuss is a philosophy of altruism. Altruism assumes
an unconditional regard for its citizens. In the ideal state of
Titmuss then, social policy to ameliorate the impact of economic
policy would be the political assumption rather than the political
debate. Rein does not agree that altruism will prevail, nor does he
see it as necessary to the function of the state. Instead Rein calls
for economic policies which will preclude the need for ameliorative
social welfare policies.

Rein refers to social welfare policy as "the poor man's economic policy" and finds it self-limiting because the "floor" of the wage structure becomes the ceiling of the benefit structure. Rein saw this as a barrier to achieving a public psychology of adequacy, a goal for the welfare state that both Rein and Titmuss support. Rein focusses his attention on the labor market to show that the nation is "juggling a problem of inequality and uncertainty in the social policy sector that belongs in the economic one" (p. 570).

The first priority of the twentieth century, according to Rein, is not equitable and equal distribution, but the debate being held in Europe and the United States on the doctrine of "overload" of the modern welfare states. This priority raises new questions on how the welfare state can be politically redefined to meet increasing social and economic obligations. Rein calls for comprehensive economic policies which are explicitly concerned with the issues of equal access and equity in resource distribution rather than separate and ameliorative policies of unilateral social redistribution. Titmuss and Rein agree that equity and equality in distribution are the criteria which will best serve to realize the goals of the mature welfare state. Rein, however, challenges the compartmentalization of social welfare with a more comprehensive approach to national welfare policy.

Rein recommends a macro/micro approach to social policy and reiterates the Titmuss call for redistribution based on equity and equality but applies these criteria to economic policies. He contends that if these principles guide the initial analyses of economic

policy, and are followed by a similar analyses of how the policies

will be operationalized to meet social welfare goals, then a cost

effective synthesis of economic and social practices around egali-

tarian values will result. He sees this as necessary to overcome the

present overload of the modern welfare states.

Occupational Welfare Based on
the Titmuss Model

While Titmuss and Rein address the broad policy issues of a

compartmentalized approach to questions of national welfare, Root

(1982), recognizing the contribution of Titmuss, focuses his attention

on gathering empirical evidence of the relationship between occupa-

tional welfare and public social policy. In a detailed case study of

the employee benefit system of the Inland Steel Corporation in Gary,

Indiana, Root makes clear the fallacy of addressing the problems of

need--either income security, health care or personal social services--

by treating social policy apart from the fiscal and occupational

benefit systems.

Root sees the crucial policy question of the twentieth century

as that of how governmentally encouraged and privately operated

welfare systems function. In his research of the fringe benefits

system at Inland Steel, he finds that the income security measures

which have emerged in the industrial settings have profound implica-

tions for national income security planning. The challenge to the

twentieth century policy analyst is to "recognize and respond to this

uneven coverage in the face of a diminished popular outcry for change"
(p. 21).

Root refers to employee benefits as a "public-private hybrid
. . . which forms a significant interlocking system of public-private
income-security" (p. 80) which calls into question the traditional
public-private dichotomy of social welfare provisions. Root found
that the fringe benefit system of the private sector had become a
substantial portion of a worker's wages and represented social welfare
benefits which stem from the employee's relationship with the
employer. These benefits came in the form of pensions, health care,
insurance plans, savings, investments and personal social services at
Inland Steel, and reflect the Titmuss contention that welfare benefits
are based on status, merit and need in the American welfare state.
The "hidden" cost of these privately sponsored programs to the
national treasury in 1981 was thirty-two billion dollars in foregone
taxes. Root questions the efficiency and the equity of this national
expenditure which benefited only fifty percent of the nation's work
force. This "contingency welfare," as Titmuss called it, is available
only if the citizen has a job, if the employer chooses to offer the
benefits or if labor is organized and bargains for the benefits as the
"union terms of agreement."

Root traces the growth of employee benefits to enactment of
the Social Security Act which established an income security base for
working people making it possible for employers to supplement this
with their own pension plans. Root, like Rein, recognized the role of

economic policy in shaping public welfare policy and found "the most enduring impact has come from the federal tax law" (p. 101).

Like Titmuss and Rein, Root found that tax considerations acted as financial incentives as a form of public subsidy which resulted in a private "enclave" of beneficiaries of the welfare state. These occupational benefits, obfuscated as social welfare, are not counted as personal income for tax purposes for the employee, and are deductible business expenses for corporations. Pension benefits in the private sector, according to Root, should be reduced by thirty-three and one-third percent if taxed as income. If Root's findings are put in the Rein framework then the "ceiling" of Social Security can be seen as the "floor" of the occupational welfare system.

Fiscal Welfare based on the Titmuss Model

Ambromovitz (1983) focuses on fiscal welfare, defined by Titmuss (1963) as the public's concern and responsibility for states of dependency among income taxpayers. Recognizing the contribution of Titmuss, Abramovitz pays particular attention to the largely invisible but expanding system of tax expenditures. When tax expenditures are combined with the traditional social welfare benefits, Abramovitz, like Titmuss, finds that "nearly everyone is on welfare" (p. 440).

Fiscal welfare in the United States is administered by the Internal Revenue Service and provides income support to individuals and families directly through tax exemptions, deductions and credits known as "tax expenditures." These expenditures are represented by exclusions, exemptions or deductions from the individual's gross income. These exclusions are in the form of special credits such as those available for child care and the preferential tax treatment of home mortgages. The tax expense system is also used to defer tax liabilities on deferred compensation in the form of pensions, and savings in the form of Individual Retirement Accounts.

Tax expenditures were first counted in 1967 when revenue foregone by the Treasury was estimated at 36.6 billion dollars or 4.4 percent of the Gross National Product (GNP). In contrast, fifteen years later, these tax expenditures were estimated at 253.5 billion dollars and 8.4 percent of the GNP. Tax expenditures for 1987 are anticipated to reach an estimated 439 billion dollars. In 1984 Congressional appropriations for ALL welfare expenses including Social Security costs, were 672 billion dollars.

A comparison of the costs of public programs through tax appropriations with the public cost of the tax expense system is instructive. It becomes evident that for every one hundred dollars spent on all public welfare through tax appropriation, the Congress expects to forego sixty-five dollars through the system of "shadow welfare" represented by tax expenditures. The one hundred dollars that is appropriated includes the universal Social Security "entitlement" programs the lion's share of which go to the middle class ("Social Security Programs in the United States," 1987, p. 7).

Ambromovitz (1983) found that corporations as well as families ask for and receive "welfare" through both direct

government outlays and tax expenditures. In 1977 and 1978 the
American Broadcasting Corporation (ABC) successfully requested
thirty-two million dollars in tax exemptions, abatements and low
interest loans even though these were years in which the company
enjoyed record profits. The Reagan Administration, according to
Ambramovitz, plans to increase federal tax benefits for industry from
the 1981 level of 48.7 billion dollars to an estimated 122 billion
dollars in 1987. Ambromovitz identifies tax expenditures with a
supplemental and concealed system of welfare, which is not monitored
or held accountable to egalitarian ideals by any designated body.

Ambromovitz's criticism of this well-to-do parallel of the
social welfare system supports the findings of Tussing (1974) as well
as Devine and Cranac (1987). The shadow welfare system she identifies raises an individual's disposable income and lowers government
revenues. She found that low public visibility of this shadow
welfare, identified by Titmuss as part of the submerged portion of the
iceberg, serves to obscure the extent to which fiscal welfare
benefits, and clearly favors, the economically privileged.

Interestingly, Ambromovitz finds that as an alternative to
direct public aid, this system of delivering benefits is relatively
generous and stigma-free. She recommends the tax expenditure system
as a more humane way to provide economic assistance. She does not,
however, discuss how the system of tax expenditures could be
structured to provide economic benefits to the financially needy who
have no individual tax liability.

Fiscal, Occupational and Social Welfare
Based on the Titmuss Model

Nelson (1983), using the Titmuss model to analyze social
policy for the aged, notes that this group benefits from each of the
social welfare categories identified by Titmuss. He takes exception
to the inequities of distribution of national resources to this
politically active constituency. He notes three tiers of benefits, of
which the public is only vaguely aware, that are available to the
elderly as categorical rights even though the aged now constitute the
wealthiest group in society.

Nelson refers to the fiscal and social welfare available to
this group by virtue of entitlements through Social Security Act and
the Older Americans Act. He fails to mention the entitlements established through the 1974 Employee Retirement Income Security Act for
the health and income protection of retired workers. Notwithstanding,
Nelson still finds that the welfare state discriminates in favor of
the elderly at the expense of society as a whole. He was critical of
the lack of program integration, fiscal planning and absence of
accountability measures in the distribution of national resources.

Nelson further notes that the Congressional Budget Act of 1974
gave implicit recognition that federal spending takes two distinct
forms, i.e., direct spending and tax spending. Nelson found Congress
had thus legitimized social action through tax acts as an accepted
alternative to the more visible statutory programs which call for
Congress to appropriate funds. Echoing Titmuss, he calls for the
establishment of a unitary jurisdiction and control of both the

direct appropriations and tax expenditures which fund programs for the aged. Such an approach, according to Nelson, would restore equity between citizens to the benefits of the welfare state, now undermined by an overemphasis on the needs of the aged.

Nelson's analysis of the programs for the aged seems incomplete. Since his analysis is based on the work of Titmuss, it might be construed that these multiple means of meeting the needs of the elderly of the nation, a class of beneficiaries most citizens can be expected to achieve, are an indication of the evolution of a sense of altruism within the welfare state. The inequities found by Nelson are real. Reframed, however, these same inequities may be cause for optimism. Could this political willingness and public consensus to act generously toward the elderly be a reflection of the nation's fifty year welfare history? Could it be that the nation's policies toward the aged signal the beginning of a cultural consensus regarding what it means to be a citizen of the welfare state? Based on the Titmuss philosophy of the welfare state, one might construe that this focus on the elderly could be the avenue by which the evolving welfare state can "find expression" for its "will to survive as a whole" through integration and harmony based on a common culture of social justice.

Social Security in the American Welfare State

While Root and Nelson analyze policy issues of special populations, Tussing (1974) takes a critical view of forty years of

Social Security in America, which he describes as a "Dual Welfare
System." He sees the American welfare state as unique in the modern
industrialized world in that selectivity in the distribution of
benefits has superseded the universal characteristics of an ideal
welfare state. Tussing found that this emphasis on selectivity has
undermined social integration within the welfare state.

Tussing, like Titmuss, found Social Security, the cornerstone of the welfare state, based on the principles of individual
achievement, status and need, creating two systems of social welfare.
The first is legitimate, implicit, invisible and non-stigmatized, a
system which provides vast unacknowledged benefits, and is represented
by Social Security. The second is illegitimate, explicit, poorly
funded, stigmatized and stigmatizing, and is represented by Public
Assistance. Tussing notes that equitable redistribution normally
implies distribution from the rich to the poor corroborating Titmuss's
finding of a public stereotype which supports this assumption.
Tussing acknowledges that this exists but found that when compared to
the redistribution within and between the middle class it becomes a
trivial phenomenon. In his opinion, national progress against poverty
will only be possible when the distinction between Social Security
and "social welfare" is eliminated.

Nowhere does Tussing acknowledge the contributions of Titmuss
but within his focus on Social Security as a dichotomous system there
is ideological consistency with the British economist as well as with
Rein, Root, and Nelson. Like Titmuss and others, he views separate

programs for the poor as typically inferior. He observes that the separation of the interests of the poor from the interests of the rest of society creates hostility between groups and diminishes the public's commitment to change.

As noted by Titmuss and Root, as well as Nelson, the greater share of welfare benefits are distributed on the basis of achievement, status and need, rather than need alone and citizenship. Like Rein and Root, Tussing noted that work is an important variable in eligibility for benefits and legitimization of welfare.

Tussing also addressed the role of tax expenditures in developing a "concealed" welfare program, devoid of any mechanism for social accountability. He noted that this concealed welfare system is not subject to annual public review as are the traditional "welfare" appropriations.

Each of these scholars calls for a "war on government benefits." However, Tussing applies this to the issue of equal and equitable redistribution within the Social Security system. He finds that welfare programs buried in tax law have an inverse relationship to need. This is consistent with Titmuss, Rein, Root, and Nelson. His work addes to the understanding of the inconsistencies which exist in the welfare state's system of redistribution. Root's research has increased knowledge and understanding of the relationship of the private system of fringe benefits (hardly "fringes" any more!) to the public welfare system. Nelson has pointed out the inequities inherent in a differentiated system and illustrates his point by analyzing programs which benefit the aged. Each of these scholars addresses issues, identified by Titmuss, that undermine the realization of the modern welfare state.

A decade after Tussing's identification of the Social Security System as a "Dual Welfare System" Devine and Canak (1986), using the Titmuss model, have quantitative evidence in support of the Tussing thesis. By a process of the disaggregation of Social Security costs in quantile shares, the investigators were able to show that welfare spending from 1949-1955 for direct relief and for Old Age, Survivor, Disability and Insurance both grew at seven percent of the Gross National Product. However, between 1955 and 1977, OASDI escalated at a rate of better than 1400 percent over the 1955 figures, while direct relief only grew by 225 percent.

The purpose of this study was to support the Titmuss contention that the now-mature American welfare state might well function to reproduce rather than transcend the existing problems of social and economic stratification. The authors found that a failure to develop a universal and integrated welfare system has had negative consequences. These consequences were the establishment of a bifurcated welfare state characterized by fragmentation, interest-group politics and an inappropriate reliance on demand-side macro-economic management, and structured to undermine democratic principles.

The authors cite the reason for this inequitable distribution as the public's perception of some beneficiaries as deserving,

represented by the middle class and American corporations, and others
as undeserving and poor. The "social expense" system, as they call
public assistance programs, is divorced from universal entitlement
based on citizenship, and delivers benefits in the form of relief to
the poor. The social consumption system, on the other hand, is a
system of universal entitlements and is represented by Social
Insurance, education, and health care.

Devine and Canak found that OASDI, worker's compensation and
unemployment insurance benefits, which serve the employable non-poor,
represented the largest share of welfare dollars. This quantitative
evaluation of the distribution of the nation's purse found that the
highly visible and politically manipulated "social expense" system
actually lays claim to very few national resources.

The Philosophical Perspective
of the Welfare State

Tullock (1983) discusses "welfare for the well-to-do" and
suggests that the basic argument of income redistribution itself has
been miscast. Tullock urges scholars to reframe questions directed at
national welfare policies to consider the political advantages that
the well-organized non-poor constituents have over the unorganized
poor constituents in the democratic welfare state.

Tullock seems to agree with the Constitutional Fathers, rather
than Titmuss, in his assessment of human nature. He found that
citizens of the welfare state are genuinely charitable to a small
extent (five percent) and genuinely selfish to a large extent. He

argues that most government programs are in fact a means of increasing the wealth of the people who are not poor. This is possible in the United States because of the nature of the Constitution and the political power of special interest groups. Like Titmuss, he finds that this political response to special interest groups by Congress serves to further differentiate the already fragmented means by which the state meets its welfare obligations. Nelson (1983) might agree since the elderly who, according to him, benefit inequitably from the welfare state, represent a well organized voting constituency in the welfare state.

Tullock found the manipulation of the government to create wealth for an organized constituency has become increasingly visible in the developed nations of the West. Economic circles refer to this phenomenon as "rent-seeking." Rent-seeking accounts for a high degree of income redistribution and is often rationalized as those policies which help disadvantaged groups.

An example of rent-seeking would be the many different programs offered to the aged addressed by Nelson. Legislators are reluctant to stem the tide of public opinion and be accused of "granny bashing" by their constituents. This gives the special interest groups such as the Association of Retired Citizens leverage with the Congress. Another example of the dual agenda of rent-seeking by special interest groups might be the health care industry's interest in having alcoholism defined as a "disease" to improve access to treatment and make the "problem" respectably "American", that is, medical. This statutory definition served to legitimize the illness, and guarantees economic and professional rewards for a new layer of "specialists" by piggy-backing a system of reimbursement already established by the medical profession and the health insurance industry. Today this entrenched medical model for the diagnosis and treatment of alcoholism is held suspect in favor of the then, as now, successful Alcoholics Anonymous community support model which is a free association of individuals.

Tullock finds special interest groups a threat to the utility of the universal franchise as a means of promoting equality among citizens within an inherently discriminatory capitalist society. These special interest groups succeed in influencing policy, according to Tullock, because neither the influential public nor the Congressional decision makers have complete and accurate information with which to formulate politically acceptable alternatives.

Tullock also finds that the welfare state, represented by the Social Security Act, discriminates against the poor. He illustrates his point with the case of the marginal worker who pays 7.51 percent Social Security payroll tax on his wages which are both low and intermittent. This being so, the wage earner can impact a very marginal Social Security benefit, since the amount of the benefit is based on income over time. Since his benefit is below the income floor of what the Supplemental Security Income pays the poor and dependent aged, his income will be supplemented to 340 dollars per month. The irony here is that this would have been available to him without any taxes on his wages over time. The worker in fact has "lost" his payroll tax, but the rest of society has gained because his taxes have been collected. Tullock also points out that Social Security Amendments have extended the worker's payroll tax to an income bracket of $49,000, thus changing repayment schedules. This served to benefit the non-poor, by allowing a higher contribution to Social Security for those well-paid employees, on which future benefits would be based.

Tullock's findings are important because they expand the menu of recommendations for policy analysts interested in a more equitable welfare state. His analysis of policy includes the traditional social policy issues, social science theory and ideological positions. In addition, Tullock identifies the emerging need to focus first on the "process" by which Congressional decision makers and the general public acquire the knowledge used to discriminate between social policy alternatives. Tullock finds the source and breadth of public information on a given issue to be of critical concern to the menu of valid choices available for Congress.

The state's greatest challenge, and the welfare state's best defense against rent-seeking are identical from Tullock's perspective. The challenge and the defense of the welfare state is the wide dissemination of correct and complete information to both Congress and the general public to undermine the power, or corroborate the validity of special interest politics.

Tullock's emphasis on the importance of the "whole truth" rather than "partial truths" is a repetition in the 1980s of a Titmuss discussion. Titmuss identified the negative impact of "commonly held but false stereotypes" on the evolution of a cultural consensus among citizens of a welfare state in "The Social Division of Welfare" (1963).

Echoing the Titmuss theme of altruism, and implying a Kenysian assumption of economic growth, Tullock suggests that to promote the potential of the welfare state, special interest groups, rather than seeking a larger slice of the welfare pie, need to concern themselves with creating yet a larger pie. He does not suggest how this might be done, nor does he recognize the "doctrine of political overload" identified by Rein (1977) as a threat characteristic of present-day welfare states.

Titmuss based his philosophy of the welfare state on the first principles of altruism and justice. He defined justice as a "respect for persons, to include reciprocity and equality in human relations" (1963, p. 215). Hacker (1985) sees little of justice in the American welfare state. His indictment is the more serious because he finds this fact neither a "perversion" nor a "betrayal". Rather he sees the development of a two-tiered system of benefits as the intent of the planners of the welfare state. He points out that the aim of the Social Security Act in 1935 was not social solidarity, but rather a response to a national monetary and employment crisis which threatened the stability of the state itself. The crisis of the depression past, Hacker finds that most middle class citizens fail to see themselves as having anything in common with the poor.

Hacker identifies the iceberg phenomenon of the public perception of social welfare. Like Tullock, he focusses on the "process" of the welfare states' political decisions. Hacker also addresses the adverse affect of a compartmentalized social welfare psychology in the minds of legislators. Hacker finds that the mature welfare state needs to include a national focus on social solidarity if the welfare society is to be realized.

Hacker calls for a "common political community," and draws attention to the Titmuss principle of altruism. He urges that the widening social class difference be arrested and eliminated by establishing the socio-economic status of the poor as the first priority of the general public. Like Titmuss, Hacker believes that to achieve the ideal democratic welfare state, society only needs to "express a certain civil spirit, a sense of mutuality, a commitment to justice" (p. 37). This is consistent with the definition of the welfare state by Titmuss as an egalitarian ideology which frames the actions of a modern evolving welfare state, rather than a set of identifiable programs mandated by statute.

Compassion and generosity are sentiments that most Americans endorse and act on only when it is a matter of bake sales and voluntary activities, according to Robert Reich, the Harvard political economist (1987). When it comes to government welfare programs, Reich finds no public consensus.

Reiterating Titmuss and the more contemporary authors, Reich
sees the economics of social welfare in America powered by a culture
which is strangled by myth. The greatest myth of all, he finds, is the
generally held myth that the American welfare state is a "Benevolent
Community." He observes that the 1980s saw a shift from a national
concern for welfare issues, to voluntary charity in the local neighborhood. He finds that volunteerism fosters "communal" value at the
expense of fostering a national community. Ironically, it was the
concept of national community, originally introduced by Roosevelt to
promote the New Deal, which gave birth to the American welfare state.
Reich finds this shift to communal values at the expense of national
community "profoundly out of sync with changing American reality"
(p. 170).

Reich finds that the tenacious and self-defeating ideology of
individualism has Americans confused regarding the nation's collective
obligation. He blames the revolt of the blue-collar and the middle-
class Americans against liberal policies, on the absence of any
acceptable shared philosophical explanation for policies reflecting
collective responsibility for the evolution of a welfare society.

Reich finds no generally understood public rationale for a
national community that will serve to buttress the concept of collective social obligation. Like Hacker (1985), Reich explains the
inequities of welfare by the fact that the majority of Americans
achieved relative economic security following the Great Depression.
When this happened, the general public began to see the "poor and

unlucky" as a separate group. Reich appears to give credence to the
Titmuss prophecy in 1958 that the critical issue in this century would
be the equitable distribution of economic resources among citizens
where rising incomes have led to social stratification.

Reich finds social welfare policy that has compartmentalized
the poor has allowed and encouraged the distance between "them" and
"us". He, too, points to the iceberg phenomenon of social welfare
and notes that hidden from public awareness is the fact that in 1985,
of the one dollar out of every nine dollars going to pay for the
general welfare (almost fifty percent of the federal budget),
eighty-five cents went to pay for Social Insurance programs. Only
seventeen cents of the welfare dollar went to pay for the programs
considered relief. In addition, occupational welfare benefits, which
he also seldom found identified as social welfare, amounted to 115
billion dollars in the same year. Reich found those benefits associated with the individual's position in the workplace cost the nation
twice as much as those programs seen as social welfare by the public.
He points to tax-free private pension benefits amounting to fifty
billion dollars in 1985 which are included in this cost. Reich found
that Social Security programs have tilted less towards bringing those
born in poverty out of that state, than to sheltering the majority of
welfare state citizens from insecurity and dependency.

Reich finds the nation's economic and social policies powered
by myth and tyrannized by stereotypes, as did Titmuss. He suggests
that the welfare state's "instruments of benevolence," designed to

59

help the poor, have been poorly conceived. Reich, like Tullock's
(1983) rent-seekers, finds that rather than serve the collective
obligations of a modern and complex society the welfare state has
served to redistribute resources among the comfortable majority.

Consistent with the Titmuss concept of a welfare state founded
on altruism and justice, Reich sees the larger question which begs for
an answer in this century as "what is the nature of the Benevolent
Community"? He sees the New Deal as having suffered less from capital
shortage and more from a decay in the capacity of the national community to collaborate in creating effective and equitable social policy
alternatives.

An analysis of the welfare state by Miller (1985) seems to be
the sum of all these scholars. He recognizes the valuable gains in
living conditions which he attributes to the welfare state and calls
for its continued development. It is interesting that he reflects the
Titmuss philosophy that a "deepening" of the welfare state is dependent on a moral will of society, and finds this collective will in
need of cultivation.

Miller does not agree with Titmuss on structural questions of
the welfare state and rejects as untenable Titmuss's view of social
policy as a separately fashioned instrument which responds to and
ameliorates the social pain inflicted by the market. Miller implies
that this atomized approach to social welfare has failed and points to
the statistics on the relative intractability of poverty over the last
fifteen years.

Reiterating Rein (1977), Miller finds the tax and transfer strategy of the welfare state fundamentally limited since the level of low wages create the ceiling of the benefit structure. Miller sees economic policy as the basic social policy and suggests that it is "the citadel of economic policy itself that must be breached if greater equality is to be achieved" (p. 62). This can only be achieved, he believes, through a combination of pro-employement and pro-poor economic policies. Unlike Titmuss, Miller is suggesting that in the modern and evolving welfare state economic policies must express social values in order for the state to impact poverty. Miller emphasizes the point that the welfare state was originally constructed on the Kenysian premise of economic growth and low unemployment. Miller finds that the new reality is that a stagnating economy has been found unable to increase the number of pieces in the Kenysian pie so that all demands can be met. He suggests that these new economic circumstances call for a change in the historic economic and social structure of the welfare state.

Miller calls for a two-pronged strategy for the future development of the welfare state. First, with thought to the basic character of American society, economic and social policy should influence the NATURE of production, which is synonymous with jobs, and so the content of the Gross National Product. In conjunction with policies on production, full employment is seen as a pivotal social policy which will do more for redistribution than the traditional transfer policies. He points out that economics is about the welfare of children and families, and that economic policy must help those who are not doing well.

In contrast to Titmuss, Miller and Rein (1977) find social policies limited in their ability to meet the needs incurred in the economic sector. Miller finds that the goals of social policy must become the goals of economic policy. Miller seems to think that economic policy, tax policy and social transfer policy must all be considered concurrently to promote equality. He suggests that the contemporary welfare state will be powered by a new theory of economics, championed by Joan Robinson and the Post-Keynesians at Cambridge University.

If Miller's prediction for contemporary social welfare is correct the implications for the structure of social welfare as a system are significant. If social welfare is to be subsumed as a goal of economic policy then this suggests a move away from the demand-side, appropriations economics of Keynesian theory, to a Post-Keynesian supply-side economics which is no longer the study of how scarce resources are allocated, but the study of how an economic system can expand to produce and distribute a social surplus. The metaphors of the proverbial economic pie can be replaced by one of a loaf of bread the size of which is dependent on the amount and nature of the yeast in the dough (Winger, 1987). See Appendix B for illustrations.

The construct for conceptualization and analysis of Post-Keynesian economic policy become those of economics as a planned purposeful activity, which is an ongoing and a cumulative process.

Post-Keynesian economics focuses on the synergistic interaction of subsystems both as a part of a larger national systems dynamic and also as a response to continual feedback from the environment (Eichner, 1979). If, as Rein (1977) and Miller (1985) suggest, economic and social policy are functionally redundant, and economic policy assumptions are changing, then change in the compartmentalized structure and function of the social welfare system of the welfare state can be anticipated.

Social policy analysts who consider economic and social policy synonymous, should note that the Post-Keynesian approach to production and distribution represents an exchange of the concept in economics of reductionism and logical analysis for that of synergism and historical evaluation in economic theory. This calls for a focus on the economic process rather than the control of economic resources. Mirroring the focus of Post-Keynesian economic theory, Titmuss refers to the social welfare process as one of social integration and social harmony realized through reductions in socio-economic discrimination in the welfare state.

Second, Miller stresses public and political attitudes towards the welfare state as crucial to what is implemented by Congress. He sees the development and spread of a moral or philosophical case for equality in the welfare state as a necessity. He observes, as Reich (1987) does, that welfare has expanded without an adequate and convincing collective argument on why that should happen. Titmuss, too, saw the importance of a collective consensus on the meaning of the

welfare state but failed to explain its absence or suggest the means
of overcoming the problem.

Summary

The Titmuss fiscal-occupational-social welfare model has
served to demonstrate the benefits enjoyed by the citizens of the
welfare state. These benefits, based on a market economy, are perva-
sive, often unrecognized by the public or the beneficiary and most
often discriminate against those who have the least status and merit,
but the greatest need.

The application of this model by these scholars for the
analysis of social policy in the American welfare state points out the
obvious. If the policies of the welfare state are to promote egalitarian ideals, then analysts must recognize and appreciate the dual
nature of the tax system which constitutes the whole purse of the
welfare state in a market economy.

These scholars call for a new definition of social welfare that
includes not only distribution through tax appropriations but distribution through the tax expense system. The findings of these scholars
show that the past failure of policy proponents to recognize the
interdependence of the dual tax systems, as predicted by Titmuss, has
led to a welfare state that has functioned to reproduce rather than
transcend existing problems of social and economic stratification.
The structure of the social welfare system proposed by Titmuss is a
unilateral system based on the concept of grants or gifts and responds

to the distress caused by the economic system. This proposed system has been challenged by American scholars.

Rein (1977) sees economic and social policy as synonymous and finds the separation of the two systems has resulted in the floor of the economic system becoming the ceiling for the social benefit system. He found that this has inhibited the development of a public pyschology of adequacy. Agreeing, Miller (1985) finds that it is "the citadel of economic policy that must be breached if greater equality is to be achieved" (p. 62). Miller notes that economic policy is about children and families, and recommends a marriage of the social welfare and economic policies such that social policy goals become the goals of the economic system. He calls for social and economic policies that are pro-employment and pro-poor to undo the threat of a two-class society. This will call for a change in the structure so that the state will influence the nature of what it is the state produced. Coupled with this change, Miller calls for a reversion to a national policy of full employment. (Maybe there is hope for the Humphrey-Hawkins full employment bill yet!)

The argument that social and economic policy be seen and evaluated as interdependent by policy proponents is reinforced by the work of Root (1982). He found the compartmentalized approach to occupational welfare undermining the social and economic goals of the welfare state. By creating an "enclave" of beneficiaries among working people, occupational social work has served to exacerbate

society's intolerance of those citizens who do not have "good" jobs
and private benefits.

The need for the definition of social welfare to include
fiscal welfare is underscored by the work of Ambromovitz (1983). She
found discrimination not only inherent in fiscal welfare but rampant,
benefitting those citizens the most whose incomes were the highest.
Adding insult to injury, the public as a whole is found to be oblivi-
ous to the fact that "almost everyone is on welfare." Because of this
"benefits oblivion" in which the citizen taxpayer lives, the welfare
state, in corporate vernacular, gets no "bang for the buck."

The very cornerstone of the American welfare state, the Social
Security Act, did not fare well under the scrutiny of the Titmuss
model for policy analysis. First Tussing (1974) and then Devine and
Canak (1987) found a social welfare system which bypasses the poor.
Their findings suggest that the structure of the American welfare
state represents a historic failure to develop the necessary precon-
ditions for democracy which must, of necessity, personalize the citizen
and institutionalize solidarity.

On the one hand, many scholars have rejected the Titmuss
concept of a unilateral system for the delivery of social welfare. On
the other hand, the principles on which Titmuss based his construct of
the welfare state are beginning to get the serious attention of
American social critics.

The foundation of the welfare state, according to Titmuss, is
altruism and reflects society's desire to survive as an integrated

whole. This serves to cultivate society's regard one for another, and the intent to serve others. Mutual regard between the state and the citizen and between citizens realizes a reciprocal purpose necessary for the welfare state to culminate in the welfare society. This Aristotelian approach to public policy has generally been ignored in favor of an empirical and determinist approach.

It might come as a surprise for the pragmatic American to find serious scholars dealing in the phenomenological a la Titmuss. Tullock (1983), who talks of rent-seeking, identified "process" as important to social policy development. Hacker (1985) calls for a "common political community" which will "express a certain civil spirit." Reich (1987) finds that the "national community" introduced by Roosevelt has been exchanged for neighborhood charity, because society has no common explanation for a welfare society's collective obligation. Miller (1985) finds that the "deepening" of the welfare state will require a moral will on the part of the citizens, together with public and political attitudes which are supported by a common "welfare society" culture.

Reich (1987) observes a decay in the capacity of the national community to create effective and equitable social policy alternatives. He suggests that the question scholars must ask is "what is the nature of the Benevolent Community"? The term decay used by Reich to describe the national community implies a full-blown presence of the welfare state. This implication is not consistent with the Titmuss view of the modern evolving welfare state. Titmuss, rather, might suggest that the United States was indeed "impregnated" and "with child" following a then ill-matched union of economic and social issues and the Social Security Act of 1935. Expanding on this analogy, one can say that the American welfare state is experiencing an unexpectedly long and more complicated gestation period than had been anticipated. This "complicated pregnancy", recognized by Reich and other scholars, has first raised questions among analysts about a "healthy delivery" for the welfare state. Second, what can Congress and the public, as "expectant parents," do to guarantee a "safe delivery"? It seems that a common culture of benevolence and a renewed moral fiber must be in place in America if the egalitarian ideals of democracy are to experience a healthy delivery.

CHAPTER III

RESEARCH METHOD

Study Design

Rationale

Information on the participation of corporations with the public sector in planning for the income security of retirees, that is, the macro-system, is available. What is not available is information on the individual corporate participant, or the micro-system. This study explores "how" and "why" decision makers respond to acts of Congress that affect the corporate design for retirement income plans.

The general objective of the study was to further inform social policy analysts as knowledge producers, and social work professionals as knowledge users. Both these groups have a professional and ethical interest in the income protection of the senior citizens of the welfare state (Reid and Smith, 1981; Weiss, 1980).

Projections for the year 2025 estimate that there will be only one hundred employees supporting Social Security benefits for every sixty-five retirees. These retirees will represent twenty percent of the population of the welfare state (U.S. Congress, House, Committee on Economic Development, Reforming Retirement Policies, 1981).

The importance of systematically analyzing public social policy, and so by implication, private sector social policies which are sanctioned by Congress, has been stated by Eveline Burns (1956):

68

. . . while there is no guarantee that democracies will act rationally in formulating their social policy, it is also abundantly clear that they cannot even be expected to do so unless they are made aware of the full implication of the choices available to them. (p. ix)

Gilbert and Specht (1974) and, more recently, Chambers (1986) expanded on the work of Burns and developed the benefit-allocation framework for policy analysis. This framework treats social policy decisions as dimensions of choice. These choices are found to be based on the best available alternatives, on values which influence the choice of the best available alternative, and on the theoretical assumptions held by decision makers.

This investigator has assumed that corporate retirement income plans for retirees are a result of individual corporate choices. It is further assumed that these choices are based on plan alternatives which are shaped by statutory policy, corporate social, economic and political values, and the theoretical constructs of the decision makers. For this reason, information on the corporate social philosophy and answers to the following questions, based in part on the work of Gilbert and Specht, became the objectives of the investigation:

1. Has tax legislation affected the income security plans that these corporations develop for retirees?

2. Who in the corporation benefits from income security plans?

3. What is the relationship of qualified defined benefit and qualified defined contribution plans to the corporate scheme of income security for retirees?

4. How are income security plans financed by corporations?

5. What are the philosophical positions of the corporate decision makers regarding income security plans for retirees?

With these questions as a conceptual framework for the investigation, it was anticipated that the relationship between acts of Congress and the corporate planning process would be systematically uncovered. In addition, this framework was expected to generate data to support the Titmuss definition of welfare that includes the fiscal and occupational as well as social categories of welfare.

Design Choices

The research design developed to logically connect the empirical evidence to acts of Congress was a hybrid. The investigator chose to couple a multiple-embedded case study of corporations with a history of the tax legislation affecting corporate income security plans for retirees, for the years of 1975 to 1985. This choice was based on Campbell's (1984, p. 9) finding that the crucial strength of the case study is the opportunity of apprehending knowledge through the understanding of historical context and the perception of patterns of response among respondents.

Multiple-Embedded Case Study

The multiple-embedded case study is recommended for data collection when little is known about a contemporary issue taking place in the real world. Yin (1984, p. 23) recommends the case study when the investigator wants answers to "how" and "why" questions about the topic to be investigated. In addition, scholars (Firestone and Herriott, 1983, p. 463) have found that the case study is an appropriate research tool when the use of the investigator as an instrument for research has utility, when the boundaries between empirical events and the context in which those events occur is unclear, and when a prior technical considerations for the structuring of a study design are not possible and must give way to "nonroutine technology." Louis (1982) found that exploratory case studies were particularly recommended when "preliminary 'knowing' is seen as crucial, where the topic in question is poorly understood, where measurement techniques are not perfected and where there is a need to identify or refine hyptheses" (p. 18).

The multiple-embedded case study provided both a strategic and a holistic way to explore the relationship of the complexly organized corporate planning process to statutory policy. Yin's (1984) case study model relinquishes the logic of sampling for that of replication. This anticipates that the same results are hoped for across each unit of analysis. This consistency in findings implies the absence of rival explanations and generates increased confidence in the results of the study. Yin defines each of the units of analysis as a single "experiment" that uncovers patterns of response and of context which allows a process of comparison between units. Yin refers to this as a "network of implication." Campbell (1984, p. 8) recommends the multiple-embedded case study as a "robust research instrument" that generates compelling evidence.

In multiple-embedded case study research it is not expected
that findings will generalize to the universe. Case studies are based
on inductive research techniques rather than deductive techniques.
The inductive techniques of the case study violate the basic tenet of
randomization and control of the hypothetico-deductive model. In the
model used here, the generation of theory through emergent concepts is
sought rather than verification of a hypothesis and a single commitment to the confirmation of transitory, if empirical, facts (Glaser
and Strauss, 1967, p. 18). Campbell (1984) has found that the well
done multiple-embedded case study generalizes to theory.

History of Tax Legislation

The history of tax legislation which offers corporate incentives for developing income security plans was incorporated into the
design to give context and meaning to the study question. Van Maanen,
Dabbs, and Faulkner (1982) and also Webb, Campbell, Schwartz, and
Schreat (1966) have written extensively on the use of external
qualitative, and non-reactive measures useful to the social scientist
when exploring the nature of something. This research design called
for a history of tax legislation designed by Congress to encourage and
shape private income security plans (see Appendix A). The investigator's purpose was to see if corporate decisions reflected the trends
in the legislation.

Yin (1984, p. 19) recommends history as an effective research
tool when an investigator has no means to access the real world of
history in the making and when the investigator is unable to exert any

control over the flow of research information. Cronbach (1980) recommends the evaluation of historical data as a means of "illuminating
the situation" (p. 11).

Limitations of the Case Study

The critical role of the investigator in case study research
can be a serious limitation. Patton (1980) has suggested that the
good investigator must emulate the habits of an athlete who maintains a
level of top physical and mental form that leads to success in compe-
tition. The case study is also threatened by the limits of the social
and technical skills of the investigator. This can result in a
limited rapport with the informants/respondents, poorly structured
questions and inadequate listening skills. Also a threat to rigorous
research in a design such as the one for this investigation, are the
investigator's organizational, communication, conceptual and perceptual
skills and biases.

In addition, rigorous case study research requires a considerable investment in time. The investigator needs to commit time for
orientation to the issue, face-to-face interviews, transcription and
documentation, and not the least, a commitment to time for just plain
thinking.

Investigator's Credentials

Between 1983-1985 the investigator served as the research
assistant for a Ford Foundation investigation of teenage paternity and
a study of corporate responsibility for retirees sponsored by the

74

Center for Regional and Urban Affairs at the University of Minnesota.
Earlier, the investigator conducted an empirical investigation of the
impact of socio-economic variables on aging.

Prior to this, a graduate school experience was an opportunity
for the investigator to become more familiar with the corporate milieu.
The investigator designed an "Employee Resource Network" in a large
insurance corporation, under the direction of the Vice-President of
Human Relations. This involved contact with the board of directors as
well as with the managers and the line employees of the corporation.
It was the investigator's contacts with the controller of this corporation that sparked interest and learning about the corporate response
to acts of Congress.

Professional experience with the health care industry
developed the investigator's sensitivity to the business community.
Social work experience as a community organizer, direct service pro-
vider and as a consultant for the Wisconsin Department of Health and
Social Services honed the investigator's organizational, communication
and data collection skills. These experiences also led to a keen
awareness of the dynamic created within an organization by acts of
Congress.

The investigator also drew on the knowledge of several experts
to improve her analytic and evaluation skills. The Director of
Taxation at Cray Research Incorporated, agreed to act as a key informant to the study. In the area of pensions, Rebecca Luzadus,
Professor of Industrial Relations at the University of Minnesota

served as key informant. In addition, the expertise of executives
from two firms which offer consultation to corporations in the area of
deferred compensation were enlisted. Each agreed to orient the investigator to the nature of qualified plans in the corporations and the
role played by tax incentives. The investigator also attended a
seminar on financial planning. At this seminar the benefits and tax
advantages were presented from the perspective of the individual
employee.

Units of Analysis

Entree to the Corporations

With past experience in the business world, the investigator
set out to survey the Minneapolis-St. Paul corporate community. The
study design called for either the Chief Executive Officer (CEO) of a
corporation or his/her designee to be the informant/respondent. This
study was not part of a larger project with an established network of
informants, nor did the investigator have any significant connections
with corporations in the Twin Cities area of Minnesota.

The investigator did, however, have the same alma mater as the
Director of the Small Business Department at the College of St. Thomas
in St. Paul. He had received considerable acclaim for his business
acumen in the Minneapolis Star Tribune, and the investigator has had
the temerity to file that information away for future reference.
Armed with the knowledge of a shared past and the promise of expertise,
the investigator requested and was granted direction on how to gain
entrance to the corporate respondents.

The alum referred the investigator to the Executive Director
of the Minnesota Business Partnership Incorporated who, in turn, suggested that she contact Allen Richie, the corporate director of compensation and employee benefits at General Mills. Richie had been and
still was, actively involved in an ad hoc capacity with Senator
Durenberger, Chair of the Senate Finance Committee studying pensions.
Allen Richie also represents General Mills in the National Association
of Private Pensions and Welfare Plans (the nomenclature of which
should interest the social work profession!).

The General Mills executive was intrigued by the study and
curiously surprised that the social work profession should be interested in corporate benefits and taxes. He agreed to be an informant/
respondent for the study. In addition, he gave the investigator a
list of compensation executives of Twin City corporations who had been
active in discussions of income security for retirees with Senator
Durenberger. These same executives were also members of the
Association of Private Pensions and Welfare Plans.

Selection of Units of Analysis

The investigator selected eight of the study informants/
respondents from the list supplied by the General Mills executive.
Selection of the units to be studied was generally dictated by
convenience, national stature of the corporation and the stature of
the corporation in the community. An attempt was made to vary the
industrial groups.

Each of the benefits executives was contacted by phone and told they had been suggested as a possible informant/respondent by his/her colleague at General Mills. After a thumbnail description of the study by the investigator, each executive was asked if he/she would partici- pate. All agreed to be involved.

A ninth informant/respondent was the Chief Executive Officer of a small paper company whom the investigator had met at a social occa- sion. The investigator had tweaked the CEO's interest in the study and he had agreed to become an informant/respondent.

Units of Analysis

The corporate executives acting as informants/respondents for their respective corporations were well credentialed. Their credibil- ity as study informants/respondents can be highly regarded considering their professional experience, their work with the legislator from Minnesota and their positions in major corporations. They held the following corporate titles: (1) Vice-President of Human Resources--Cray Research, Incorporated; (2) Vice-President, Compensation and Benefits-- Dayton-Hudson Incorporated; (3) Corporate Director, Compensation and Employee Benefits--General Mills Incorporated; (4) Corporate Benefits Administrator--Honeywell Incorporated; (5) Pension Manager--Minnesota Mining and Manufacturing Company; (6) Director, Employee Benefits-- Pillsbury Company; (7) Director of Compensation--Super Valu Incorporated; (8) Director, Tax Accounts--Toro Incorporated; (9) Chief Executive Officer--Wilcox Paper Company. All these corporations are

Minnesota "born-and-bred" and have their headquarters in the Twin
Cities of Minneapolis and St. Paul, Minnesota.

Cray Research, Incorporated, founded in 1972, was the youngest
of the companies to be studied. The company's mission is to design,
manufacture, market, and support the most powerful computer systems
available. Cray Research supercomputers account for approximately
two-thirds of the worldwide installed base of these high-performance
systems. Cray Research belongs to the industrial manufacturing group,
is publicly owned, and employs about four thousand people. The
average age of employees is thirty-two with an average service tenure
of 2.5 years. Of these, sixty percent are women and forty percent are
men (Annual Report, 1985).

The study informant/respondent, Gene Johnson, Vice-President,
Human Resources, was thirty-nine years of age with a degree in
Industrial Relations and seven years of service with the company.

Dayton Hudson Corporation is a growth company with a focus on
retail sales. In 1985 the company operated 1,206 stores in forty-eight
states, the District of Columbia and Puerto Rico. The company's
mission is to provide exceptional value to the American consumer
through Target, Dayton Hudson Department Stores, Mervyn's and specialty
merchandisers. Dayton Hudson belongs to the consumer products industrial group, and is publicly owned. Dayton Hudson contributes five
percent of its federal taxable income to support giving programs.
According to the 1985 annual report, Dayton Hudson believes the

"return on investment (ROI) is the most important single measure of financial performance and is the primary tool we use to manage our business." The 1985 goal for ROI was 16.2 percent.

The study informant/respondent, Fred Hamacher, Vice-President, Compensation and Benefits, was between the age of fifty-five and sixty-five, and had been with the corporation for twelve years, and had credentials in business management.

General Mills belongs to the consumer products industrial group, is publicly owned, and has a total of fifty-five thousand employees. The average age of salaried employees is forty-three with eight years of service. The corporation focuses ninety percent of its resources on consumer foods and restaurants. These represent the company's highest return and fastest growth areas. Two of the most visible of General Mill's divisions are Betty Crocker Foods and the Red Lobster Restaurants. The corporation added forty-five new restaurants in 1986 compared to four in 1985. This focus represents a historic restructuring of the corporation which took place in 1985. With this emphasis on consumer foods and restaurants, General Mills couples a small presence in specialty retailing, represented by companies such as Eddie Bauer.

The corporation is committed to competitive excellence and maintaining a leadership position in its field. The corporate management routinely teams with private foundations in the community in planning ways to serve social needs (Annual Report, 1985).

The study informant/respondent, Allen Richie, Corporate Director, Compensation and Employee Benefits, was between the ages of thirty-five and forty-five, had a Masters in Business Administration and had been with the company for twelve years.

Honeywell Incorporated is a member of the industrial manufacturing group and is publically owned. Honeywell employs sixty-five thousand people in the United States and about ninety thousand worldwide. The average age is thirty-eight among salaried employees with eight years of service. Honeywell prides itself on the fact that "many of our executives have spent most, if not all, of their working careers at Honeywell" (Annual Report, 1985, p. 3). Among organized employees the average age is 42.5 and the average tenure is ten years.

1985 represented the one-hundredth anniversary of service in business automation and control, and also represented the company's focus for the future. Since 1982 Honeywell has sold two hundred million dollars in nine businesses that did not fit their "core". Ventures and acquisitions to the future will be designed to support business automation and control. The corporation expects to take advantage of the synergy of its holdings and of the emerging customer demand for integrated computer, communication and control systems (Annual Report, 1985).

The study informant/respondent, Howard Amborn, Corporate Benefits Administration, did not have advanced academic credentials, had spent the last twenty years of his working career in benefits management and was between the ages of fifty-five and sixty-five.

Minnesota Mining and Manufacturing (3M) is a worldwide company serving customers with a broad range of innovative, high-quality products and services. The company employs eighty-five thousand people and has operations in forty-nine countries. The company is publicly owned, with forty-nine thousand employees in the United States. The average age of these employees is forty and average tenure is ten years.

3M considers its hallmark to be the practice of sharing technological information in order to build businesses. Corporate business is organized around four sectors: Industrial and Consumer, Electronic and Information Technologies, Life Sciences, and Graphic Technologies.

This corporation takes pride in a working climate that is designed to encourage employees to find new and better ways of doing things. 3M accomplishes this by assuring employees that the company is willing to take risks, is supportive of innovative ideas and at the same time recognizes that not all new efforts will succeed (Annual Report, 1985).

The study informant/respondent, Ron Schutte, Pension Manager, was between the age of thirty-five and forty-five, had an academic degree in business education and a specialty in actuarial science. He had been with 3M for ten years.

The Pillsbury Company is a diversified, international, market-oriented organization and belongs to the restaurant and packaged foods industrial group. Pillsbury is publicly owned, has a total of 110,000 employees, thirty thousand of whom are full-time career employees. The average age of employees is 35.8 years with 7.9 years of service.

Pillsbury takes pride in supplying premium quality foods products and outstanding service to customers as well as a superior return to stockholders. Well known divisions of Pillsbury include Pillsbury Foods, Green Giant Foods, Steak and Ale Restaurants and the Burger King fast food chain.

The company expresses a commitment to outstanding citizenship as a member of the community and in creating an environment for employees that makes Pillsbury an exceptional place to work. The corporate philosophy states that "people make the difference, quality is essential and excellence must be a way of life" (Annual Report, 1985, p. 5).

The study informant/respondent, George Rux, Director, Employee Benefits, was between the ages of thirty-five and forty-five, had a Masters in Business Administration, and had been at Pillsbury for eight years.

Super Valu Incorporated is a food wholesaler and also offers retail support services to its customers. The corporation is publicly owned, belongs to the wholesale retail industrial group and has twenty-five thousand employees. The average age of the employees at Super Value is less than thirty, and average tenure is three years.

The corporate mission is to serve customers more effectively than anyone else in its field. Super Valu employees at seventeen retail support divisions serve over three thousand independently owned food stores in thirty-two states. A rather recent addition to the Super Valu portfolio is Shopko, a non-foods mass merchandise operation which operates fifty-nine stores in seven Midwest states (Annual Report, 1985).

The study informant/respondent, Robert Shebick, Director of Compensation, was between the ages of thirty-five and forty-five, had a Master in Industrial Relations and had been at Super Valu for five years.

Toro Incorporated is a world leader in the manufacture and marketing of equipment that offers labor-saving solutions to the problems of outdoor maintenance. The corporate focus is on both residential and commercial equipment. Toro employs about two thousand people, who average about thirty-five years of age and have an average tenure of ten years with Toro.

Corporate success is sought in ways that do not involve assuming a great deal of debt, but without sacrifice to the responsiveness of the corporation to both the consumer and the commercial marketplace. Toro insists on product excellence for its worldwide market of lawn, snow removal, and turf and turf irrigation equipment. In 1985 the corporate sales were twenty percent higher than in 1984. This represented the third best year since the company was founded in 1913 (Annual Report, 1985).

The study informant/respondent, Gary Bartolett, Director, Tax Accounts, was over forty years of age, is a Certified Public Accountant, and has been with Toro for thirteen years.

Wilcox Paper, in business since 1923, was the smallest company in the study, and is privately held. Wilcox Paper belongs to the industrial distribution group, employs forty people with an average age of thirty-eight to forty and average tenure of eight years. Of all employees, two percent are wage and hour, seven percent are organized, and ninety-one percent are salaried.

The study informant/respondent, Dick Mast, Chief Executive Officer, was over fifty, held a Bachelor of Arts Degree, and had been with Wilcox Paper for eleven years.

Study Etiquette

Respondents were sent letters on University of Minnesota stationery, thanking them for their willingness to participate in the study. In this letter, the investigator was identified and information made available on how to contact her if necessary. Also, the letter identified the doctoral student's advisor as a reference, and urged them to contact the University if they had questions about the study. See letter and accompanying study prospectus in Appendix C.

Having spent years in a government bureaucracy, the investigator was aware of the gatekeeping and information and referral role played by the secretaries of executives. Whenever possible, the investigator established a personal network by building rapport with the secretaries. In this case, the secretaries were all women. Each of them expressed an interest in the study, although the degree of interest varied.

Data Collection

The collection of data for this study was a three-stage process. First, the investigator developed a legislative history of the tax acts that impacted corporate income security plans between 1975 and 1985 (see Appendix A). Armed with this information and the rigorous orientation of the investigator to the subject of corporate retirement income plans, first and second face-to-face interviews were scheduled with each of the participants to complete the three-stage process. During the initial guided interviews the participants were in the role of informants. The second set of interviews involved the administration of a semi-structured survey instrument. The participants were then in the role of respondents (Yin, 1984).

All study informants/respondents were asked for permission to record the interviews. All but one agreed, who claimed an unwillingness to be "quoted". The ability to tape record interviews freed the investigator to concentrate on the discussion and to probe more judiciously. Transcription followed the interviews as soon as possible. The time invested in each interview and the transcription averaged about eight hours. The structure of the interviews, implicit in the initial guided interviews, and made explicit in the interview schedule, simplified the information coding process.

The Open-Ended Interview

Initially, two-hour face-to-face guided and open-ended interviews were held with each of the corporate decision makers. These interviews served to build rapport between the informants and the

investigator as individuals. Rapport was also developed at the conceptual level. The investigator introduced the executives to the
subject of retirement income protection from the perspective of a
social work professional. The informant was then given the opportunity
to be involved in structuring the survey instrument for the study, in
his capacity as a informant to the investigation (Yin, 1984).

The investigator guided each interview to cover corporate
philosophy and policy regarding the income security of retirees. Also
covered in this initial interview were the designs of each corporation
for the protection of retirement income. In addition, informants were
encouraged to discuss the corporate response to the individual acts of
Congress in question. The focus of these questions was on the impact
of the legislation on the corporate plans and the integration of
qualified corporate plans with Social Security benefits.

During this initial interview, each informant was asked to
supply copies of the corporate Summary of Plan Description (SPD)
required annually by the Internal Revenue Service (IRS) to clarify
corporate qualified plans for employees. Also requested were copies
of the IRS form 5500 for the years 1978 and 1985. This form is the
official corporate report on qualified plans required by the IRS and
the Department of Labor. (This did not apply to the one corporation
in the study of less than one hundred employees.)

At the end of each session the investigator requested a
second two-hour interview. The informants were advised that the
investigator would develop a semi-structured survey instrument based on

part on information, speculation, attitudes and theory shared by the informants. Appointments for the second interview were made at that time. All informants agreed to be study respondents in the second phase of data collection. Letters to the informants followed the interview to express appreciation for their commitment of time and expertise. This letter also served to confirm the date and time of the next interview.

Semi-Structured Survey Interview

The semi-structured survey schedule was grounded in the data collected from the first open-ended interviews, the legislative history and the information gleaned from a review of the literature and the investigator's orientation by compensation professionals. The instrument included open-ended and closed questions as well as a series of questions with fixed answers from which respondents could choose. The administration of the instrument took approximately two hours. The investigator was forced to probe with discipline in the interest of time. The investigator was sensitive to verbal and nonverbal cues from the respondents regarding an infringement on the time agreed upon. The investigator used the "focus interview" model (Patton, 1978, p. 77) where the instrument is not shared with the respondent, and is made as unobtrusive as possible to simulate a "conversation".

The instrument covered information on the corporate plans for retirement income, plan participation, eligibility for benefits, vesting schedules, plan finance and the administration of the plans. Respondents were asked for information on their perspective on future initiatives in corporate qualified plans, their philosophy regarding the relationship of economic and social well-being, and the corporate policy regarding retirees. Other questions focused specifically on those benefits seen to be indices of corporate response to acts of Congress, such as Payroll Stock Option Plans (PSOPs) and the 401(k) savings plans.

The instrument also addressed the explanations that appear to rival acts of Congress as the variable around which retirement plans are developed (Campbell, 1963). The investigator considered the following explanations: (a) the human relations factor, (b) corporate recruitment needs, (c) corporate social responsibility, (d) organized labor's terms of agreement, (e) attention to the competitive position of the corporation, and (f) tax incentives. The last page of the instrument covered the corporate demographics, planned so that if the investigator ran out of time, these data could be easy to collect by telephone later. See Appendix D for copy of this instrument.

At the end of the final interview each respondent was asked if he would like an executive summary of the research report, and whether or not the investigator could call on him to answer further questions. In each case the answers to the questions were in the affirmative. Following the final interview the investigator sent a second letter again expressing appreciation for the executive's contribution of time and expertise to the study. See letter to General Mills in Appendix C.

History of Corporate Tax Incentives

The investigator explored the primary sources of the legislation between 1975 and 1985 that addressed corporate qualified retirement income plans. The Congress's manifest intent with legislation of
this nature is to encourage corporations to develop income security
plans with tax incentives, while simultaneously shaping and regulating those plans. The investigator looked for trends in the legislation which might be harbingers of change in Congressional focus
regarding the desired corporate response. This analysis of the
legislative policies and trends was collated with response of the
corporation to the legislation.

The following pieces of legislation were reviewed and
analyzed: (a) the 1974 Employee Retirement Income Security Act for
background information, (b) the 1978 Revenue Act, (c) the 1981
Economic Recovery Tax Act, (d) the Tax Equity and Fiscal Responsibility
Act of 1982, (e) the Deficit Reduction Act of 1984, and (f) the
Retirement Equity Act of 1984. See Appendix A.

Comments in Retrospect

The study called for the informant/respondent to be at the
administrative level. Implicit in the design was the assumption that
the same person would be both informant and respondent. The importance
of both these requirements was brought out in an incident at 3M. When
the investigator arrived at 3M at the appointed time for the second
interview, she was informed the respondent had had to leave town
unexpectedly the night before. However, he had arranged for a

replacement from his staff. The interview was a disaster. First, there was no immediate rapport. And second, not being in an administrative position, the replacement was unable to answer questions on the philosophy of the corporation. Nor was he familiar with the corporate history of retirement plans. Also, he was unable to comment for the corporation, nor could he comment on the intent of Congressional action, from the perspective of the compensation professional. What the investigator got was the "public relations" pitch on 3M's concern for the retiree and the line-manager's exalted opinion of his superior! The original informant graciously agreed to reschedule the meeting.

A second incident points out the pitfalls for the inexperienced investigator in developing the units to be analyzed. Marshall and Isle of Milwaukee, the largest bank in Wisconsin, had been referred to the investigator through the Alumni Foundation of the University of Wisconsin as a corporation with a very avant-garde approach to deferred compensation planning. The contact with the appropriate person was made, the study explained, and an appointment made for an interview. In the interest of time and distance, the investigator decided to use the telephone for a shortened first interview. The semi-structured instrument was mailed to the respondent so that she would be aware of all the areas to be covered in the two-hour interview. This was a mistake! The informant/respondent called and cancelled her involvement with the study on the grounds that discussing such sensitive information was against company policy. It was disappointing to the investigator because of the promise of finding an innovative design for retirement plans. The lesson learned is that there is a point at which the investigator uses caution regarding how much information is shared prior to building that critical sense of confidence between the participant and the investigator.

Validity

Apparent Validity

The discussion of validity in qualitative research, according to Kirk and Miller (1986) and Yin (1984), is organized around apparent validity (face validity) which assumes instrumental and theoretical validity. Apparent validity has to do with the "currency", that is, the value of the findings yielded and the utility of the instrument for generating data. Apparent validity also is concerned that the variables be correctly labeled.

The data collection procedures in this study had a high level of currency due to the calibre and experience of the participants as well as the sound theoretical grounding of the investigator. The amount of time, four hours apiece, that the participants were willing to contribute was also a significant factor in the currency of the findings. Also, the value of the data collected was enhanced by the predetermined structure of the initial interviews. The semi-structured survey instrument, by its nature, ensured a certain level of currency. This, too, was in part a function of the credentials of the participants of the study.

Several steps were taken to make sure that the variables were correctly labeled. Key informants with expertise in taxes and pensions were enlisted to act as consultants. Also, the literature on corporate pensions was searched. In addition, the nomenclature of the variables was validated by the participants themselves.

Instrumental Validity

Instrumental validity (construct) is concerned with the ability of the research instrument to collect data which will serve to validate and generate the theoretical propositions of the study. In this case, certain income security plans, sanctioned by acts of Congress, such as the 401(k), and certain policies, such as the integration of Social Security and the corporate pension plans, served as indicators of corporate response to legislation. The semi-structured survey instrument included questions on corporate participation in all the retirement income benefits plans sanctioned by the legislation over the decade of the study. This fulfilled the requirement for instrumental validity that the evidence be empirical.

Further, Coleman (1972) has made it quite clear that those who analyze social policy in the real world of action engage in a discussion and a frame of reference quite different from that of the theoretician and analyst. He suggests that new knowledge is incomplete without input from this distinct set of decision makers and stakeholders.

Theoretical Validity

This study of the corporate response to Congressional tax incentives was designed to demonstrate the utility and reliability of the Titmuss fiscal-occupational-social model for the identification of what constitute social policy in the welfare state. The study was designed to demonstrate that this broad definition of social welfare on which Titmuss based his model has validity for reconceptualizing "welfare" in the modern welfare state to include corporate employee benefits, that is, occupational welfare.

Pensions plans sponsored by employers have long been encouraged by public policy. Private retirement income benefits are seen by Congress as a necessary part of the national plan for the income protection of those citizens over sixty-five. Pension legislation has been called a social purpose Act by Titmuss. It can be assumed that corporate income security plans demonstrate one means by which the welfare state has chosen to protect retired citizens from economic dependency. These corporate income security plans, encouraged by Congress and supported by public dollars, would therefore be a valid indicator of occupational benefits as welfare.

To reinforce the Titmuss frame for identifying welfare, the study methodology adapted the benefit-allocation mechanism developed by Gilbert and Specht (1974). This modified framework organized the data according to the allocation, provisions and financing of occupational benefits. By imposing this traditional structure for social policy analysis on the collection of data, a comparison between social welfare represented by the tip of the iceberg and the occupational welfare of private pension plans was conceptually available. The similarities of purpose, that is, the alleviation of man-made dependencies, is demonstrated by the findings of this study. The similarities of purpose served by public and private benefits lends credibility to the utility of the Titmuss model for policy analysis and validity to his broader definition of welfare.

Reliability

The case study method has in the past been criticized for an inability to guarantee reliability. Louis (1982) and Baltzell (1980) recommend what they call the "standardized case method" to overcome this weakness. Louis recommends the two-stage data collection procedure used in this study, when preliminary "knowing" is seen as crucial.

Phase one was used to develop knowledge, rapport with the informant and establish the parameters of the study. The second phase led to the development of an instrument formed on the data base of phase one, and reflected participation by the informants, key informants, and the primary sources of pertinent legislation. This two-stage procedure is recommended for generating comparative data for a cross-case analysis of the multiple-embedded case study.

The open-ended interview was guided by an implicit structure around the variables of the study and initiated the data collection. For the second phase of data collection the investigator used a semi-structured survey instrument developed around the variables of the study. These instruments are considered appropriate and effective for the collection of specific facts in case studies by both Yin (1984) and Kirk and Miller (1986).

Babbie (1975) has suggested that a standardized measure used to explicate information when the topic is complex can be like "fitting a square peg into a round hole" (p. 346). He had found that the threat to reliability of the untested measure can be offset with a sophisticated analysis of the data. This research design compensates for the lack of boundaries often found in case studies. The investigator structured data collection within a standardized framework for social policy analysis. The topics within these established boundaries are those recognized by scholars as pertinent to social policy analysis and are congruent with the Titmuss model.

The study questions were organized around the specifications identified in the study rationale. The study rationale, in turn, was based on the theoretical propositions of the study. This gave the instrument cosmological cohesiveness and integrity in relation to the study question, as well as a high level of consistency in the data that were generated.

Yin (1984) sees the formalization of questions in certain case studies as "not only a necessary step, but a sufficient one" (p. 55). The structure employed in this study led to a precise language for describing the findings and reporting on "pattern development". This level of precision would have been more difficult to achieve if the investigator had been reactive rather than proactive in the interview situation. The nature of the instruments of this study also generated data that established study credibility through the cross-sight agreement found between units.

All the interviews were conducted by this investigator. Nor did the participants in the study change. This consistency served to further minimize threats to reliability. All but two of the eighteen interviews were recorded. Annual corporate reports were secured to corroborate descriptive data. The IRS form 5500 was designed to serve as a reliability check on the study variables. The Summary of Plan Description procured from each of the informants/respondents served the same purpose, and was easy for the "lay person" to understand. Field notes and tape recordings of the interviews are available for use by other scholars.

The history of Congress' tax acts was based on primary sources. This history, besides being pertinent to the study question, also served as a reliability check on the "network of implications" as they evolved during the investigation.

Threats to the reliability of the study were also minimized by keeping the design practical. That is, the study was financially possible and do-able by a single investigator, with limited time, working outside of a formal project. The study proved feasible in that access was gained to corporate decision makers who were very knowledgeable, helpful and interested in the question.

The ethic of the study was maintained by the investigator's commitment to report findings with integrity.

Limitations

The strength of a case study is found in the logical link of
the findings with the theory upon which the study is based. Titmuss
did not develop a theory of the welfare state to support his model of
analysis of social policy. Hence, he offers no systematic direction
to the change agent. This study refers instead to major assumptions
which are consistent throughout his writings.

The absence of project funding posed limitations. Financial
resources would have allowed a research design for more scope for
investigating this timely question. Funds would have allowed time for
additional follow-up. In addition, if technical assistance had been
available, more of the investigator's time could have been used for
data collection. Also, project funds would have allowed the investigator to take fuller advantage of this opportunity to work with
leading corporate executives in the private benefits field. This
well-informed group of corporate compensation managers have a great
deal of historical and current information, as well as insight on the
trends for the future that could have been more fully exploited.

If the investigator were to redesign this study, the major
adjustment would be with the semi-structured survey instrument. To
obtain objectivity the "price" paid for the "currency" of the data was
relatively dear. Since this instrument was central to the design for
data collection, the criticism is important.

The informants/respondents were well informed, competent and
seasoned professionals with a great deal of information at their

fingertips. The investigator quickly became aware that the participants took much pleasure in being "informants". What was realized in
retrospect was that the participants as "reactors" both responded less
elaborately and also seemed less challenged by the interview. Judging
from the high level of currency achieved in the first unstructured
guided interviews, this investigator would recommend that other
scholars who may be interested in similar research design the second
instrument so that the role of "informant" is maintained in preference
to that of "respondent".

    A semi-structured survey instrument that used only open-ended
questions plus the demographic questions would have fit this situation
better. In addition, the investigator would be much more selective in
constructing the questionnaire. Some of the information yielded by
the survey instrument was already public information (IRS 5500) or
could have been inferred from a combination of information from the
Summary of Plan Description and the taped interviews. The elimination
of unnecessary questions would allow more time for probing and mutual
understanding. The quest for objectivity in this case was misguided.

CHAPTER IV

CORPORATE RESPONSE TO LEGISLATION

By the year 2000 it is expected that one out of five Americans will be over sixty-five years of age. The income security of this group is a concern to Congress. At the present rate of births and population growth, the American employers and employees will be required to support sixty-five pensioners for every one hundred workers through the Social Security Tax. This is putting employers in a very responsible position in Congress' scheme for the income security of retirees (U.S. Congress, House, Select Committee on Aging, Future of Retirement Programs, 1987).

Since passage of the precedent-setting Employee Retirement Income Security Act (ERISA) in 1974, Congress has attempted to encourage, shape and regulate the allocation and provision of corporate employee benefits for retirees. The manifest purpose of Congressional action is the development of the well-balanced income security "stool" for the nation's retirees. The first leg of that stool is considered Social Security and Supplemental Security Income; the second, private pensions; and the third leg, individual employee savings and investments.

This chapter will discuss how and why nine corporate decision makers responded to acts of Congress that impacted their retirement income security plans between 1975 and 1985. The corporate response

99

to five acts of Congress will be discussed chronologically. This
discussion is followed by a report on the retirement income plans
these corporations offer their employees. Finally, the writer discusses the rival explanations for the corporations' response to these
acts of Congress.

The Revenue Act of 1978

The Revenue Act of 1978 was precedent-setting legislation.
For the first time Congress extended special tax incentives to the
employee as well as the employer for participating in a plan for
income security. The 401(k) has made saving money popular in these
corporations because of the extraodinary incentives offered by
Congress. For the first time, the employee is entitled to tax-free
earnings. This benefit is contingent on the employee's willingness to
save.

The employee pays no tax on the dollars as they are saved via
the employer-sponsored 401(k). There is also no tax on the investments accrued from these savings during the working years. In addition, at retirement the savings are taxed at the traditionally lower
rate that applies to the individual's retirement income tax bracket.

Dayton Hudson and Pillsbury were the first to get on the
401(k) bandwagon in 1982, following by Toro in 1983. General Mills was
the last to respond in 1985. Only Wilcox Paper did not offer this plan
to their employees. The Chief Executive Officer (CEO) at Wilcox Paper
was advised against putting such a plan in by the corporation's benefits
consultant. The deferred compensation specialist felt that Congress'

incentive would be rescinded with the tax reform because "it was too good to last." This incident was an example of the importance of "process" and the attendant damages of incomplete information to the realization of welfare goals, as pointed out by Tullock (1983). It is worth noting, also, that of all the corporations in this study only Wilcox Paper did not employ their own legal staff charged with the difficult responsibility of keeping abreast of changes in tax legislation, the Internal Revenue Code and "case law" which might affect the corporate revenue picture.

The Hardship and Loan Features of 401(k)

To add to the employer's enthusiasm for this savings plan, withdrawals are allowed, without a tax penalty, in cases of certain personal hardships experienced by the employee. This flexibility, absent in the Individual Retirement Accounts (IRA) encourages the participation of the lower level employees who have less discretionary income. It should be noted too, that the participation of these lower level employees is critical to the "qualified" status of the plan. The list of hardships considered legitimate are diverse and include, but are not limited to, at one extreme a home destroyed by fire and at the other, extraordinary medical needs.

Employers can also develop loan features for the 401(k) in which case the employee is borrowing on personal capital. In addition, the interest paid on these loans is tax deductible. This means that an employee is, in a sense, paying interest to himself or herself.

Only Dayton Hudson, 3M and Pillsbury offer 401(k) loans to their employees. The experience of these corporations with loans has been positive. The initial reason for adding a loan feature was their confidence that the employees would put the money back into their deferred savings account, given the convenience of payroll deductions. They have not been disappointed. Also, these informants felt that the loan feature encouraged young families to take advantage of the incentive to save tax-free dollars without giving up the financial elasticity often needed when discretionary income is limited. Those corporations that do not have a loan feature based their decision on added administrative costs and a philosophical position where they perceived loans on savings in the present defeated the purpose of saving for retirement.

Employer Discretion

It is worth noting that it is these corporate decision makers who choose whether or not employees have the advantages of a loan feature, based on their value judgments. There are no "union terms of agreement" because only unorganized employees qualify for this tax incentive. In the case of this study the corporate choice seemed in part based on the decision makers' attitudes about the wisdom of allowing the employee self-determination, and the decision makers' loyalty to the concept of "retirement security" as opposed to income needs in the present.

The 401(k) as an Addition to Earnings

The informants pointed out that for many employees the 401(k) yields a greater tax deferral than an Individual Retirement Account (IRA) which is limited to two thousand dollars. Also, for those who can afford it, a 401(k) can be used in addition to an IRA. This makes this savings plan particularly attractive to the employee who has discretionary income. In this study, those identified as having discretionary income were both the key employees and the "second earner" employee whose spouse was the primary bread winner.

According to Amborn at Honeywell, the 401(k) is

a very good deal--costs the corporation to develop and administer but gives employees an excellent financial break via taxes. We are planning to add a loan department.

In these corporations the 401(k) payroll savings are not considered a reduction in the employee's take-home pay, as is generally expected from payroll savings accounts. Rather, this savings plan represents an ADDITION to earnings when company matching contributions and the tax advantage to the employee are considered together. In those cases where there is no company match it is still possible for the employee to contribute to a 401(k) and have an increase in take-home pay. The 401(k) thus allows the sponsoring employer the opportunity to increase real wages at the government's expense! Also, because of the many attractive features of the 401(k) these decision makers use this savings plan as an employee perquisite. That has not been true of the traditional payroll reduction "thrift plans" which are offered by employers as a convenience rather than a "perk" or benefit.

To clearly show the financial advantages of a 401(k), the schedule from the Cray Research Summary of Plan Description (SPD) is presented in Table 2. This SPD gives a graphic illustration of how the 401(k) can work for the employee. An understanding of these advantages implies a real need for all employers and all employees to fully understand what this plan can do for them, at Congress's expense.

TABLE 2

SCHEDULE FROM CRAY RESEARCH
SUMMARY OF PLAN DESCRIPTION

Example	After-Tax Saving	Before-Tax Saving
Annual pay	$ 20,000	$ 20,000
Before-tax savings	-0-	-800
Taxable income	$ 20,000	$ 19,200
Federal tax (estimate)	-3,200	-3,008
After-tax pay	$ 16,800	$ 16,192
After-tax savings	-800	-0-
Estimated take-home pay	$ 16,000	$ 16,192

Employee contributions to the 401(k) are immediately vested by statute. That is, the employee becomes entitled to the benefit when the contribution is made. This is important to the employee who chooses to terminate employment because accrued savings and interest can be withdrawn without penalty. On the other hand, for the employer interested in retention of employees, the 401(k) will only be useful to the degree that the employer contributes! This is in contrast to pension benefits which are withheld to encourage employee retention. Immediate vesting qualifies the 401(k) as a portable employee benefit. That is, a benefit that will not be lost to the employee because of a change in employment.

In these corporations the employee also had the privilege of leaving the accrued assets in the corporate investment trust, so that the investment portfolio would go undisturbed. The vesting schedules for employer contributions in this study ranged from zero to five years. This compares very favorably with the vesting schedules for pension benefits which now range from five to seven years. In addition, pension benefits are prorated over a thirty-year period, with the highest return realized in the last five to ten years of a thirty-year career. With the 401(k) the employer's contributions are now made annually. At Cray Research both employer and employee contributions are fully vested immediately. Commenting on the restructing of their plan, Johnson said

> We had a vesting schedule before that was complicated and stringent and we didn't know why we had it, and then we decided with all this planning we're going through let's get rid of it. . . . Why say we give you this contribution and then only let you have half of it when you leave the company?

Corporate Response to the 401(k)

Cray Research introduced the 401(k) in 1984. Johnson said of their decision, "We could take advantage of that and we hadn't been doing it and it was a real nifty thing."

Dayton Hudson's Hamacher said:

It was one of those things that sounded too good to be true. I don't think anyone knew what it was. We were the earliest retailer to have a 401(k) by far. Ahead of Sears, Pennys or any of them. It was a sleeper, I don't remember any discussion back . . . if I'd heard the concept . . . I'd have jumped on that one quick . . . because it makes a hell of a lot of sense. Because I always felt there was never incentive for people to save money, always incentive for people to spend.

All the informants were enthusiastic about 401(k)s and the reception of the concept by employees. At Dayton Hudson employee savings went from twelve million per year to forty million per year. According to Hamacher,

We wrote it up, I went to the directors, they asked a couple questions, I went back the next week and we approved it. Took us two weeks. Because they said this is the right thing to do, and we're going to do it. We showed all employees how they could participate and have the same take-home--what company money would amount to in five or ten years. The numbers go up quite dramatically.

At Honeywell Amborn reported that they did not adopt it sooner because they were unable to convince the directors of the advantages. It is interesting that at Super Valu it was the need to remain competitive with other employers that led them to offer the plan to their employees. At Pillsbury, Rux contended that it "makes economic good sense to have employees save their own money for retirement and other purposes."

Interestingly, according to the executive of Dayton Hudson, half of the employees who contribute the maximum allowed to the 401(k) are the lower-paid employees. The informant suggested that, contrary to public opinion, the "second earner" who can save a high percentage of salary does exist. He also was of the opinion that the 401(k) is popular because people have an innate desire to save.

> The IRS will say, 'That's just for the high-paid people.' They're wrong . . . you can't get it through their damn heads. They think these plans operate in a discriminatory manner and they don't.

This suggests that these corporate employers are aware that personal savings will be needed to supplement Social Security benefits in retirement if they are to live in the manner to which they have become accustomed. In addition, it is significant that Congress seems to have developed a successful mechanism for encouraging a savings ethic among employees that is attractive to these corporate decision makers.

At Cray Research, the informant found that employees were much more financially sophisticated than a decade ago. Amborn at Honeywell agreed. "I have people who push brooms who are sophisticated investors." The informant from Toro has found that employee interest in saving is much higher than when he came to Toro. In his opinion, "We are in a savings age." Congress would be pleased to hear that! This informant has found that "they [employees] have never known 4.5 percent interest. The great American dream comes at 10.5 percent now. . . . They need to save."

Congress' price tag for this tax incentive is corporate compliance with the IRS standards of eligibility and discrimination in
the plans for corporate participation. That is, employers were
obliged to offer the same opportunity to an equitable proportion of
lower-paid employees within the corporation as a contingency for the
participation of the higher-paid employees. Offering the opportunity
is not enough, however. These corporations are also required to
demonstrate that participation by employees in the saving plan is, in
fact, in proportion to the standards set by the IRS, for that group
of employees, which, in the case of this study, are the "salaried
employees".

The 401(k) and Early Retirement

Uncertainty has been created among the corporate decision
makers in this study by the 1982 Tax Equity and Fiscal Responsibility
Act (TEFRA) and the Deficit Reduction Act (DEFRA) of 1984. These
informants are questioning whether or not Congress will continue to
give pension trust funds a preferred tax status.

A combination of events has made the question of retirement
one of first importance. Changing public demand, changing technology,
changing demographics of the employed population, and changes in some
cases, in the focus of these corporations has led to a proactive
corporate policy on early retirement; that is, early retirement is
being actively encouraged. According to the respondent at General
Mills, "No one retires at sixty-five anymore." At General Mills
eighty percent of the employees take an early retirement. At

Honeywell, "normal" retirement has been reduced to sixty. At Super
Valu forty-nine percent of the employees take early retirement.

Congress's decision to narrow the range within which income
would qualify for tax-favored deferred compensation has made retirement less financially attractive to the upper-level employee in these
corporations. The benefits which in the past bridged the gap between
early retirement and the onset of Social Security benefits are now
more often than not taxable to the employee. This reduces their value
as income to the employee. This also negates their value as a
corporate perquisite. The compensation managers are being forced to
develop new incentives for early retirement or continue to keep the
employee on the payroll. This can prove to be expensive for the
corporation if the position filled by the employee has become obsolete.

Congress's tax disincentives for the development of pension
plans have served to make the 401(k) doubly attractive to employers.
As the executive at Dayton Hudson explained

> One of the reasons for doing this [instituting a 401(k)], was
> that if there were pressure on pensions to go upward through
> forced retirement pension increases, this would be our justifica-
> tion to say, 'No, we're not going to do that.'"

At General Mills there is no reduction in benefits for those
employees who take an early retirement. This incentive explains why
eighty percent of their employees retire early. General Mill's early
retirement policies, according to the informant, were developed in the
1960s. Richie questioned the validity of the policy today, "whether
we would do that again in the current environment is doubtful . . .
people live and work longer." In addition, following TEFRA these

prospective early retirees will not be enjoying the same tax advantages on discretionary income as their forerunners.

These informants see the 401(k) as a cost-effective means of supplementing an employee's early retirement income in the absence of other tax-favored benefits. The 401(k) allows corporate employer contributions of up to seven thousand dollars annually to the employee's savings in tax-free dollars. In addition, the upper-level employee has a new statutorily approved and significant tax shelter for discretionary income.

Discussion

The 401(k) savings plan can be seen as legislation that has successfully addressed the self-interest of the welfare state which is capital formation. This is a benefit which employers use to attract and retain employees who want tax shelters for discretionary income. And the employee can now save earnings before paying taxes and can enjoy quite a dramatic increase in income over time. Tullock (1983) refers to use of government policies for personal gain as rent-seeking. In the case of the 401(k) where the interests of all parties are served, rent-seeking becomes legitimized.

The welfare state's interest was, in this case, to encourage capital formation among employees so that the nation's income security programs for retirees will be viable in the future (U.S. Congress, House, Committee for Economic Development, Reforming Retirement Policies, 1981).

The interest of the corporate employers in this study was served when Congress designed a financially efficient perquisite with which to attract and retain those employees who was tax shelters for discretionary income. In addition, through the 401(k) the nation's employers were able to offer lower-level employees the opportunity of increasing their income at the cost of the federal government, rather than the employer.

The employee's self-interest was served with the Revenue Act by the opportunity to increase income at the expense of the government through personal savings, based on tax-free dollars. Further, the employee was given the security of knowing that the accrued savings would be available in the event of an unanticipated change in the personal financial picture.

This legislation establishes the concept of "income security" in exchange for "retirement security" by applying the concept to include working and post-work life's events. Congress has, in a sense, redefined income security to include both retirement income security and income security during the employee's working years.

Important to the employee considering income security in the future is the fact that the 401(k) contributions cannot be included in salary calculations of retirement benefits. The benefits accumulated through the 401(k) mechanism are to be considered personal savings, not "pension" benefits. Ironically, the enthusiasm of the corporations for the 401(k) may prove problematic to the lower-level employee. Employer contributions to the employee accounts are sometimes

perceived as "retirement benefits" and equated with the defined
benefit plan, seen only as more flexible. However, as a retirement
"benefit" from the corporation, 401(k)s are a cheap substitute, if
compared with the defined pension benefit. Drucker (1976) has made
clear that investments and savings are two different animals. Pension
plans are an investment in the future and are protected as such. The
401(k) is a savings plan and a hedge against bad times, with no
built-in protections. Employees need to be very clear about what the
employer and their own contributions to these various plans mean, in
order to have optimum "income security." The sturdy three-legged
stool that Congress uses as an analogy for retirement income security
may end up with one short leg, or worse, only two legs.

The 401(k) is a significant financial benefit for all levels
of employees. It is a benefit which is subsidized heavily by Congress.
However, employees cannot benefit from these tax incentives unless
their employer chooses to sponsor the plan. On the other hand, all
employees, in fact, "pay" for this tax-favored savings plan through
their personal tax liabilities.

Given that the 401(k) serves the interest of the employer as
well as the employee, it seems that Congress should guarantee the
right of the nation's employees to participate in this revolutionary
savings plan.

The 1981 Economic Recovery Tax Act (ERTA)

Individual Retirement Accounts (IRAs)

ERTA, noted for restructuring the national tax system, reaffirmed Congressional interest in capital formation at the national level and savings at the individual level. The Individual Retirement Accounts of 1974, with their attractive tax feature, became available to all citizens, regardless of whether or not they were covered by an employer retirement income plan. In addition, Congress raised the dollar limit for individual contributions to two thousand dollars from fifteen hundred dollars annually, deductible up until April 15 of the following tax year.

Only three of the corporation in this study offer their employees IRAs. The comment has been that there is "no sense in offering an IRA, now that we have a 401(k)." The corporations that do offer IRAs--General Mills, Honeywell and 3M--do so as an employee convenience. Also, according to the informant from 3M, so that employees can benefit from the large investment pool at 3M. With IRAs available at credit unions and banks, there was little pressure or incentive to formally include IRAs in corporate design for retirement income. The advantage of the IRA is that it is a tax benefit available to all citizens (within a certain income bracket, if they have an employer plan, since the passage of the Tax Reform Act in 1986) who have income to save. The one advantage of the IRA over the 401(k) is that participation in this post-work income security plan is not contingent upon employment and the discretion of the employer.

However, it is employment that most often afford those individuals who need income protection in old age some discretionary income for savings!

Employee Stock Ownership Plans (ESOPs)

Employee Stock Ownership Plans have been a favorite with Congress for a long time. Since ERISA the ESOPs have been blessed with tax incentives that are not available to other qualified plans. ERTA allowed permanent payroll-based tax credits for employer contributions to a tax credit ESOP.

ERTA made ESOPs more attractive to employers by basing the annual tax credit allowed the company on a percentage of the employer's payroll instead of a percentage of the company investments. After ERTA the Employee Stock Option Plans became a means to raise capital by a corporation through wages and salaries that were deferred, making this benefit very attractive to employers as well as employees (Ludwig and Curtis, 1981). ESOPs encouraged the corporations to include more employees so that the tax credit would be greater. A key feature of ESOPs was the requirement that employees who become stockholders also enjoy corporate voting rights, thus democratizing the workplace.

The manifest goal of this legislation was to encourage the nation's economic recovery in a period of economic stagflation, by structuring an attractive means to finance corporate expansion. Concurrently, ERTA fostered the ownership of American companies by American workers. The latent goal of Congress in sweetening the

corporate incentives for ESOPs (P.L. 97-35) was to encourage corporations to keep their companies in the United States, hire American
workers and, of course, collect Social Insurance taxes and broaden the
individual tax base.

ESOPs, like the 401(k), also represent that ideal situation
where the self-interest of the state, employee and the employer are
served. Despite the attractiveness of the ESOP, only Toro has structured its income security plans for retirement around the ESOP. This
option is suited to labor-intensive organizations and, of the corporations studied, Toro most closely represented this category. The informant at Toro was proud of what he perceived as a participatory form of
management which "offered opportunity to employees rather than
promises."

Payroll Stock Option Plan (PAYSOP)

It is instructive of the power of tax incentives to note that
all the corporations but two did subscribe to the time-limited Payroll
Stock Option Plan which was initiated by ERTA and scheduled by
Congress for expiration in 1987. PAYSOPs were more suited to the
demographics of these publicly held corporations and cost the corporation nothing. PAYSOP was a payroll-based tax credit but the employee
receives this in cash rather than stock, as in the ESOP. No
"ownership" by employees is involved. As one informant said, "It's a
tax credit. I might as well give it to the employees as the government." For the profitable corporation, the credit is subtracted from
the corporate tax liability and divided evenly among all employees.

The CEO and the clerk enjoy the same benefit. When Congress offers tax incentives such as the PAYSOP it pays to be employed by a profitable corporation! Described by one informant

> On the one hand I like them, on the other hand administration
> is a monster with our kind of company, with 130,000 people and high
> turnover, administration is a killer. Rather than paying Uncle
> Sam $25,000,000 we give it to the employees ($70-$90 per year).
> It's very 'efficient' to give that benefit to the employees.
> Each gets the same, the Chairman gets the same as the salesperson.

The entire cost of a PAYSOP was born through the tax expense system via corporate tax credits on liability. For the employee, the benefit is deferred to normal retirement age and represents an investment in retirement income. This "free lunch", as the informants called PAYSOP, however, was only available to those who were employed and to those employees whose employers chose to participate. The cost of the benefit, on the other hand, was of course borne by all taxpayers.

Discussion

The compensation professionals in this study refer to this period between ERISA and ERTA as the "era of compliance." Although these corporations had preempted many of the standards of ERISA, adaption to the new statutory policy was administratively difficult. The informants reported that corporate-wide educational programs were necessary. Employees needed assurance that the new regulations would not affect them adversely. The publicity on ERISA that informed the general public tended to address situations where employers were not serving the best interest of the employees. It is ironic that those corporations that had preempted much of the law were required to spend time and effort, which is money in the corporation, reassuring their employees that their retirement income plans would not be undermined.

ERISA and subsequent legislation has required that corporations become socialized to the concept of government control of private income security plans for retirees. This era of relative quiet from 1975 to 1981 was followed by the dawn of the Congressional "era of freedom for rational benefit planning" as Shebick of Super Valu called it.

1982 Tax Equity and Fiscal Responsibility Act (TEFRA)

The Revenue Act of 1978 set a precedent by allowing a tax advantage to employers and employees who saved a portion of their wages. The Tax Equity and Fiscal Responsibility Act also set a precedent. For the first time in the history of Congress, legislation was enacted which served to limit the development of corporate pension plans for retirement. The era of freedom for corporate income security planning begun with ERISA came to an end with TEFRA, according to one respondent.

Most of the corporations in this study did not see this legislation as a trend initiated by Congress to limit the development of qualified defined benefit plans. The informants saw TEFRA rather as a bill to collect revenue in response to public pressure over the national budget deficit. At Super Valu, Robert Shevick commented that "if the federal thrust has in the past been to increase the number of

118

pensions, new legislation is simply to raise revenue." Also, the
corporations saw TEFRA as a means for Congress, following passage of
the distinctly pro-business Economic Recovery Tax Act in 1981, to
improve their public image of fairness in taxation.

The changes mandated by TEFRA affected all qualified retirement plans. TEFRA restricted the absolute dollar contribution by the
employer for defined benefit plans to $90,000 down from $136,425 and
limited corporate participation in officer-defined contribution plans
to $30,000 down from $90,000. These "top-heavy" rules affected tax-
favored deferred compensation for employees in the upper echelon in a
significant way.

Addressing the new top-heavy rules, Fred Hamacher of Dayton
Hudson, who had only one officer who "topped out," complained that
TEFRA was politically motivated window dressing by legislators. "Tax
equity and fiscal responsibility, how can you vote against that?
That's done for show."

Allen Richie at General Mills, however, shared that in his
company "many officers have topped out." On the other hand, speaking
in somewhat the same vein as Hamacher, Richie suggested that Congress
had passed TEFRA "to impress the public that they were out to get the
fat cats." Having said that, however, he allowed that

> TEFRA has taken away the federal subsidy on what Congress
> deemed excessive benefits. The social limit for subsidy is now
> $90,000. However, not many people in that bracket [but admittedly
> quite a few at General Mills!]. Congress appealed to each other--
> needed legislation which would pass--in terms of revenue the
> amount gained is insignificant.

According to these compensation professionals it is mathematically impossible for the large corporations to discriminate in favor of highly compensated employees. The qualified plans require that participation and compensation be actuarially determined. To be disqualified by the IRS, top-heavy plans must represent more than sixty percent of the aggregate benefits in a given corporation. As the informant from Super Valu pointed out, in a corporation of five thousand there would probably be twenty-four key employees. It would be quite impossible for these twenty-four employees to hold sixty percent of the tax-qualified benefits.

The CEO of New Era Financial Planning, a key informant for this investigation, supports this position. He suggests that TEFRA was aimed primarily at smaller corporations where deferred compensation is more likely to be used as a tax shelter.

> In smaller corporations tax incentives are a primary motivator. The larger the company gets the more diffused is the ownership . . . spread out . . . no concentration of a few people trying to create benefits for themselves . . . large companies . . . a sense of public responsibility . . . employee morale . . . retention . . . image. The bigger the company the more important are these factors.

The financial limits placed on qualified plans to defer compensation for highly paid employees has meant that corporations have gone to "nonqualified plans" which are not pre-funded and are taxed as income to the employee. The employer still deducts the corporate cost as an expense and, as a bonus, avoids the discrimination rules of "ERISA plans" and the PBGC costs. However, these advantages come at the price of a popular perquisite for key employees. Dayton Hudson,

General Mills, Honeywell, Pillsbury and Super Valu all have both non-qualified benefit and contribution plans for their upper-level employees.

The Dayton Hudson executive expressed frustration with Congress. At the same time, he mitigated the impact of TEFRA on his corporation and suggested that the legislation was directed at small companies where "key" employees were "raking it in."

> It's really a mixed signal, on the one hand ERISA comes along and make you appropriately protect the rights of the people [with funded plans]. Then they turn around and start limiting it. I've got people right now that are young, that are in their early thirties, and making a substantial wage that are going to hit the limit. I'm going to have more and more people under current law, and a huge number under the new tax law [1986] that are going to hit the maximum--so now I've gone from a properly funded plan to a plan which will be unfunded. That's a big signal I think.

This move to nonqualified plans means that beneficiaries will not be covered by the ERISA standards or have the protection offered by the Pension Benefit Guarantee Corporation. These key employees will bear the full risk of corporate takeover or bankruptcy.

Congressional Definition of Eligibility for Benefits

Given the remarks by these informants, the social significance of TEFRA does not seem to be in the potential for revenue collection. Rather, this Act's significance seems to be in the Congressional definition of who is eligible for social purpose dollars. That is, who among employees needs to have retirement income subsidized by the welfare state.

Viewed in the long term, however, if the number of employees in the upper brackets are growing, as suggested by some of the informants, then the savings of social purpose dollars will compound. Concommitantly, the reduction of tax-sheltered plans will broaden the tax base. In addition, it is significant, in a time of market uncertainty, that Congress has successfully avoided possible financial responsibility for generous corporate pensions through the PBGC. If the sponsors of retirement income for upper-level employees default on their promises it could be assumed that these employees will have adequate means for helping themselves.

Another more obtuse effect of TEFRA, but equally as important, may be to encourage employers to find ways to reward key employees that will not be based so directly on the status and merit of market criteria. TEFRA has undermined the market value of these benefits by removing the Congressional tax subsidy. Employers, known to respond quickly to market advantages and disadvantages, may be encouraged to seek rewards for key employees which are based on other criteria. Possibly altruism? TEFRA may be a means for establishing career goals based on social values rather than upward mobility and increases in wages. Miller (1985) alluded to this when he referred to the need to consider the nature of production if economic goals are to reflect social values. TEFRA points out that "money" in the present, when considered in relation to tax liability, seems to be losing its value to the upper echelon.

The Corporate Value System

To fully understand the corporate perspective on deferred compensation, it is important for the social policy analyst to understand that retirement income security plans are developed by these corporations first as an incentive to attract and retain key employees. All employees are important in the corporation but the pool from which key employees are drawn is smaller and, so, more competitive.

It is also important for the social policy analyst to understand the conceptual framework of the business ethic. Retirement income protection needs are always based on a percentage of pre-retirement pay that is expected to meet the economic demands of retirement. Level of pay becomes an objective measure of the employee's standard of living. Retirement plans are designed to maintain that standard of living.

The corporations in this study reward employees in proportion to what the employee and the employer have contributed to Social Security. Also considered is the employee's service contribution to the corporation. The assumption is that the higher the level of pay, the greater the aggregate contribution by the employee to the corporation. The corporate ethic requires that the greater the employee's combined contribution the greater should be the corporate reward in retirement. The rational market criteria for the distribution of resources or "rewards" support this measure as equitable and just within corporations.

The difference between market criteria and the criteria of altruism are apparent when discussing the importance of maintaining the employee's standard of living with the corporations in this study. As one informant explained it, "As income goes up, the need for additional savings [deferred compensation], the other leg of the stool, becomes more important. It's important at all levels but it's much more important at the upper level."

Implicit in this approach to measuring need for retirement income is that the lower-level employees have not been accustomed to a high standard of living in work years so they do not need it in retirement.

Market Criteria Versus Adequacy

It is interesting that Titmuss addressed the need for the welfare state to reject market criteria in favor of criteria based on altruism and justice if economic and social inequities between citizens were to be avoided. If the corporation is looked on as a model of the modern welfare state it becomes readily apparent, on analyzing TEFRA, that a system based on status merit and need compounds differences between people based on their relationship to employment. This problem can be exacerbated by Congress, as pointed out by Tussing (1974) and Devine and Canak (1987) in their findings on Social Security, as well as mitigated by Congress, as in the case of TEFRA.

The wisdom of the Titmuss criticism is clarified if the distribution of benefits that result from Social Security in the corporation and TEFRA are compared. Social Security targets social benefits based on need and earning power. TEFRA now has targeted social benefits based on the concept of adequacy. The assumption can be made that TEFRA targets the social purpose dollars to those employees with more economic need. This raises the thought-provoking question of whether the welfare state has an obligation to be equally as generous with public dollars to those who have economic means as to those who do not. TEFRA has based the distribution of resources on a range of incomes deemed adequate for retirement, rather than on need, status and merit. This is both target and cost effective and narrows the gap between the haves and the have-nots.

When viewed through the lens of a corporation, it seems clear to this writer that the welfare state should support adequate retirement income protection when there is a need with social purpose dollars. Conversely, those who have adequate economic means should support the welfare state by CONTRIBUTING social purpose dollars! This is the meaning of reciprocity as perceived by Titmuss as well as Hacker (1985), Miller (1985) and Reich (1987).

In light of Rein's (1977) findings that all modern welfare states are buckling under the "doctrine of overload" the time seems right to question the concept of "universal" as presently defined, and replace market criteria with a measure of adequacy. There seems to be sufficient evidence that the market criteria of need has obfuscated the meaning of social and economic distribution as symbolic of the modern welfare state. Distribution in the welfare state was intended to alleviate man-made dependencies, not promote man-made advantages between "them" and "us", as articulated by Reich (1986).

The Corporation and Integration

In fairness to the corporations, Congress has a history of support for these market criteria. In collusion with the conservative public and with employers, Congress has santioned a 50 to 70 percent income replacement standard as adequate income protection in retirement. Congress has also sanctioned the integration of corporate income security plans with Social Security benefits. This has allowed employers to contribute less to the retirement of their lower-level employees and more to higher-level employees based on expected Social Security benefits. This arrangement has recognized the inverse relationship of costs and benefits realized by both employee and employer, as well as the benefit levels of Social Security. The informants in this study complain that Congress is systematically underming the practice of integration.

The integration of Social Security benefits with private income security plans was seen by Congress and these employers as a means of restoring equity to the market system. This rationale makes little sense since all Social Security beneficiaries are estimated to have consumed what they have paid into the Social Security within their first thirty-six months of retirement.

Employers have long been socialized to this concept of equity, aided and abetted by Congress. The average citizen, a product

of the workplace and proponent of market criteria, also sees this as
equitable, having been socialized to market criteria.

Corporate Ire

Relatively speaking, this investigator was given the impression that TEFRA is considered more an administrative irritation by
these decision makers than a significant cost. However, while TEFRA
is seen as partially irrelevant to these corporations, it is perceived
by these decision makers as grossly unfair. The corporate ethic of
fairness measured by market criteria is very objective and very strong
among the informants in this study.

Since TEFRA, the employee who pays a high Social Security tax
will now also pay a high tax on unqualified employee retirement
benefits. The new regulations also deny the employee the benefit of
the special tax forwarding clause on personal tax returns awarded
qualified deferred compensation. Qualified deferred compensation
enjoys a five-year forwarding clause for the tax bite for those under
fifty years of age and ten-year forwarding for those over fifty years
of age.

The bad news for the highly compensated is that nonqualified
deferment could represent a considerable tax penalty. The good news
for Congress is that the employees who "top-out" are in the upper
income bracket and will not go hungry. In addition, TEFRA will serve
to broaden the base of the personal tax system and increase revenue
over time. That is, TEFRA will serve to increase instead of decrease
the national tax purse. From the social policy perspective TEFRA has

guaranteed a more equitable and socially effective use of the national social purpose dollars.

TEFRA and Early Retirement

TEFRA has adversely affected early retirement benefits in all these corporations except Wilcox Paper and Cray Research. An actuarial limit based on age sixty-two rather than age sixty-five Social Security standards became the point from which corporations could compute downward to establish early retirement benefits of fifty-five year-old employees. This has the effect of limiting the use of "qualified tax dollars" to encourage early retirement.

If employees can choose whether or not to retire, it can be assumed that those who do not retire will continue to pay into the Social Security system, and also pay a personal tax in a higher bracket than if they had retired. Discouraging early retirement would serve both the Congressional need to stay the drain on Social Security assets and also broaden the personal tax base. The benefits to the state would be compounded.

It is interesting to note that the business community in Washington, D.C., to stay a Congressional move to mandate corporate pensions, lobbied for increased opportunities in employement and benefits for workers over sixty-five as a compromise. The result was the Old Age Discrimination Act with attractive tax advantages for workers over sixty-five years of age. At the same time, however, "back home on the farm," employers were and are encouraging early retirement (Levitan and Cooper, 1984)! If these corporations are typical of large corporations across the country, Congress might well be concerned about the effect of corporate early retirement policies on both Social Security assets, the nation's personal tax base and the waste of human resources.

All these early retirees will be eligible for Social Security and medical benefits at age sixty-two or age sixty-five. Their contribution to the national purse, however, will have been limited by retirement from paid work that is taxed for Social Security. Also, the reduction in income of the employee will result in a reduction of individual tax contributions. On the other hand, the benefits these early retirees receive will not be affected. The question is raised as to who IS responsible for supporting the aged dependent? Should it only be one class of workers? Should it be the young workers who are raising families and have less discretionary income for the purpose or should it be all citizens who have the means? Should certain classes of people be rewarded for choosing not to participate in the support of the welfare state? It hardly seems proper that Congress should aid and abet, through social purpose dollars, a corporate program which so severely undermines the distributive capacity and the resources of the welfare state.

TEFRA and the Structure of the Pension System

TEFRA also changed the structure of the pension taxing system. Prior to this legislation, the individual retiree and the IRS negotiated the tax liability. After TEFRA, the individual discretion on tax liability was curtailed when the pension fund trustee and these employers became accountable for withholding the appropriate taxes on the pensions of retirees. This adds administrative burden to the corporate defined benefit plans, and effectively ties these employers to promises as they come due, systematizes the process for the IRA and makes pension plan information more accessible to the public and Congressional oversight. This is congruent with the Congressional thrust for increased awareness on the part of employees and employers of costs and of occupational benefits.

Discussion

Titmuss urged the welfare state to model the ideals of the egalitarian state so that citizens could be socialized to the "welfare society." TEFRA focusses on adequacy in the distribution of social purpose dollars. The new Congressional controls exercised over the distribution of resources in corporations may be a means of socializing the marketplace to the concepts of economic and social adequacy in collective welfare, that is, fiscal-occupational-social welfare. Rein (1977) and Miller (1985) both agree that for the goals of the welfare state to be realized economic policy must adopt social goals. Congress seems to have moved the corporations studied here in this direction with TEFRA. Devine and Canak (1987) refer to this as the "social consumption system." All of these scholars saw the lion's share of the welfare state's resources going to the well-organized middle class. TEFRA represents an effort by Congress to limit the ability of citizens to benefit from rent-seeking.

The 1984 Deficit Reduction Act (DEFRA)

The Deficit Reduction Act (P.L. 98-369) followed on the heels of TEFRA in 1984. The stated purpose of this act was to reduce the national budget deficit and to halt the erosion of the nation's tax base. With this legislation Congress continued to focus on limiting and regulating the development of corporate retirement plans. In the words of the informant from General Mills, "It's DEFRA which really caused the problem . . . limited prefunding . . . a negative piece of legislation. Intended to raise fifty billion in revenue to reduce the deficit."

DEFRA did not make life easier in the corporation! The corporate welfare trust funds invest tax-preferred dollars to support health and life insurance benefits for employees. Congress now has imposed a tax bite on all trust assets in excess of ten percent of the present corporate liability. In addition, the corporate contributions to "funded welfare" on behalf of key employees is not tax deductible if the plan is found to be discriminatory by the IRS. Also, the trust benefits were more narrowly defined to include only life and health benefits and exclude any benefits which could be construed to be deferred income.

Traditionally, these corporations have used attractive life and health insurance policies as perquisites to attract and retain key employees. DEFRA limits the corporate tax deduction for the prefunding of the funded welfare benefits to retired employees. On the other hand, employee contributions to funded welfare are fully tax deductible through cafeteria plans.

Interestingly, DEFRA introduces a new wrinkle and a new incentive on the subject of integration to these corporations. Now corporations can integrate the privately funded welfare plans for disability income coverage with public sources of diability income. This reduces the costs to these corporations and represents a new "sharing" of responsibility between the public and private sectors for those who are disabled. The disabled employee is also entitled to a tax credit on the individual tax liability for this benefit.

DEFRA, like TEFRA two years earlier, is forcing these decision makers to look for new cost efficient perquisites to enhance retirement income security of upper-level employees. The decision makers are constrained in this search by the fact that many attractive tax and investment advantages for the funding of these benefits no longer exist, plus the employee advantage of funded welfare benefits discounted as personal income have evaporated (Section 79, DEFRA).

Section 132 of the Internal Revenue Code provided that all fringe benefits are taxable income to employees with the exception of four categories. The final guidelines for cafeteria plans (the preliminaries came in 1980) were issued requiring employees to pre-select benefits a year in advance in order to benefit from pretax dollars. Cafeteria plans were designed to more effectively target resources to employee needs and control corporate costs. Cafeteria plans were also designed to raise the sponsor's and the beneficiary's awareness of the cost and the utility of health benefits.

DEFRA excluded benefits in the form of deferred compensation from cafeteria plans except for the 401(k) savings plans. To support the Congressional goal of encouraging informed decisions on the part of consumers of benefits, DEFRA allowed preferential tax treatment for employers who offered preretirement planning programs to their employees.

The informants pointed out that employees accustomed to comprehensive health coverage are at risk of making poor choices and also at the risk of unknown future circumstances. This will limit their effective use of tax-free dollars for health care and, under some plans, may even result in unncessary cost to the beneficiary through assigned dollars which go unused.

It is interesting that Titmuss (1963), Tullock (1983) and Hacker (1985), as well as other scholars, find correct and complete public information to be the best defense against practices which undermine the development of egalitarian ideals. Congress, in enacting DEFRA and giving preferential tax treatment to employers who offer pre-retirement counseling to employees, seems to agree.

Employee Trust in the Corporation

Major changes imposed on these corporations by Congress in areas such as pension benefits and health policies affect individual employees directly. The disruption of the employee/employer trust dynamic requires management reassurance that changes will not affect the corporate population adversely. The informants for this study were all proud of the trust held by employees for the corporation. One informant said, "You do things differently if you are a company like ours. It depends on the corporate philosophy. Some just 'kick ass and take names so to speak.'"

The frequent legislation has not only imposed administrative and financial burdens on these corporations, but also the burden of maintaining the employees' trust in the organization in response to externally imposed social and economic policy changes.

Employee Protections

DEFRA continued the Congressional recognition of the needs of employees. The employer's right to terminate retirement income security plans is now regulated. The plan assets must now go first to satisfy the employer's promised obligation to those who are presently retired as well as those employees with vested pension benefits.

Welfare Trust Funds

DEFRA also issued stringent new regulations to control the financial assets held in "funded welfare" trusts; that is, those trusts which fund medical and health costs of employees. DEFRA now taxes as corporate income all welfare trust funds in excess of ten percent of the funds needed to meet estimated expenses. This is significant for corporations such as 3M who incur ten million dollars annually in health and insurance costs. However, over the years the company has built a trust which, through investments, takes care of the health and medical obligations of the employer plan. In the language of DEFRA,

> Deferred compensation rules [special tax treatment rules] do not apply to welfare benefits if those benefits are not regarded as deferred compensation . . . if an expenditure results in the creation of an asset having a useful life which extends substantially beyond the close of the taxable year such an expenditure may not be deductible, or may be deductible only in part, for the taxable year in which made or incurred. (Treasury Regulation, Sec. 1461-1(a)(1)(2))

Ron Schutte at 3M reacted to DEFRA as one who had been betrayed. His department has been considered a national model for the pre-funding of corporate benefits. According to Shutte, 3M has acted as a consultant to many companies anxious to emulate 3M's plans for funding of postwork life insurance and medical plans. With the passage of DEFRA 3M suddenly became the culprit rather than the ideal model. In his words,

> 3M and IBM are unique in that they established medical and life insurance trusts for the purpose of meeting retiree obligations. We thought it prudent. Our costs run about ten million dollars but the trust is taking care of these costs. Unfortunately under DEFRA we are no longer able to contribute to this trust, cannot be in excess of the legal limit. Can only have enough in the trust to cover current expenses. The irony of the situation is that the Financial Accounting Standards Board has been saying 'do as 3M does'--and now we will be taxed.

In response to the investigator's question on what action 3M would now take, the informant said the situation was still "being negotiated with the IRS." It is a fact worth noting that corporations and the IRS negotiate the definitions of such terms as reasonable, excessive and equitable in relation to the individual corporation. According to the informant at 3M, "We negotiate interpretations with

the IRS. Certain revenue rulings must be lived by . . . often difficult to interpret."

This individuality can be both an advantage and a disadvantage, depending on the corporate relationship with the "street level
bureaucrat" from the IRS. Rapport between the corporation and the
particular IRS office serving the company is important. The corporate goals and history give context to the tax decisions and affect
their interpretation by the IRS. The corporation with a poor community image for fairness and ethics in business will be unlikely to get
the same level of unconditional regard for the corporate rationale as
the corporations with an unsullied business reputation.

At General Mills, Richie elaborated on the intention of
Congress in passing DEFRA and offered increasing the tax base as a
very plausible explanation for the new restrictions on business.

> If Congress thinks caps on health care deductions will create
> an urge on the part of companies to control health care benefits--
> that's a pipe dream--just the opposite will happen--if health care
> can't be deducted--we will give each employee two hundred dollars
> more per month and they can find their own. There are four
> people down the hall working on health care who won't be needed--
> we won't pay them and will be $200,000 ahead. That's what the
> government wants because they want to broaden the tax base--a
> Repulican kind of approach.

The taxing of the excess assets in the funded welfare plans
has the corporate community frustrated over what seems like inconsistencies on the part of Congress. After years of encouraging
employers to offer employee benefits, Congress has reversed its
position. This has not served to build a sense of confidence in
Congress among these decision makers.

Informants are speculating about the future action of Congress in relation to pension trust funds. If Congress should decide to restrict the corporate pension trust funds the informants would need to reevaluate the existing corporate policies on income security in retirement. Present practices would lose their value to the corporation as cost efficient and socially effective means of supporting private income security plans for retirement.

Discussion

All the corporations in this study had pension funds with excess assets. All the informants were concerned about the employer's social obligation to protect the retiree's standard of living. Each informant in those corporations with pension plans were currently agonizing about the trends which they perceived in Congress to limit the tax preferred funding mechanisms for employee benefits.

The investigator came away with the impression that pensions were considered a sound social and economic benefit by these informants. At 3M Schutte said, "We know if we give people more money they will not save for retirement." Changes in the corporate direction that reduce the role of defined benefit plans in the income protection of retirees will not come without considerable debate.

It was very important to these corporations that the community perceive them as good and equitable employers. Defined benefit plans offer the corporations a controlled way of preserving their image of social responsibility. One informant, with a shade of indignation, said, "Corporations can have social goals, just because you're a

corporation doesn't mean that you don't have social concerns." The
informant from Dayton Hudson shared that, "The last thing we want is
to see Dayton employees on welfare because there is no pension plan
or medical plan . . . bad press."

All the informants considered the existing employees nonforfeitable pension assets an employee "entitlement." One informant was
careful to define entitlement to conceptually separate an existing
plan from the concept of corporate obligation to offer a defined
benefit plan to employees. In response to the question, "Do you
consider the qualified defined benefit an entitlement?", he responded:

> No, I don't think so . . . I don't think any program is a
> 'right' . . . there is no statutory requirement that you have to
> offer . . . Congress in the last of the ERISA legislations made it
> very clear that you needn't offer pensions but, if you do, then
> there are protections. So, clearly, in this country it is not a
> statutory right.

Predictably, none of the informants thought the excess assets
of the pension trust funds belonged to the employees, while all did
agree that pension benefits were "deferred wages." All the informants
agreed that "in the case of excess assets, they should accrue to the
benefit of the employer." However, Schutte of 3M shared the information that this was an area that was under discussion, and getting
close scrutiny by the Federal Accounting Standards Board.

A major concern for these corporations is an anticipated
assault by Congress on the pension trust funds similar to the assault
on funded welfare trusts in DEFRA. These corporations have all been
very successful in financing the defined benefit plans through the
investment assets of the trust funds.

From the perspective of the employee, it might be said that
the employer who sponsors a pension plan does in fact manage the
employee's own deferred wages, while being reimbursed for his trouble
with the interest accrued on the employees' wages!

The Retirement Equity Act (REA)

The Retirement Equity Act (P.L. 98-397) set yet another
precedent by establishing marriage as an economic partnership. REA
also removed sex and age as barriers to career goals. The long-term
social significance of this act cannot be overstated in light of the
egalitarian goals of the welfare state. REA mandates that these
corporations recognize the unique social differences in career
patterns between men and women while, at the same time, mandating that
the measure used to allocate the benefits be androgynous.

Titmuss (Wilding, 1976) found that social policies of the
welfare state should be responsive to the changing roles of women and
to society's changing burdens of dependency. This responsiveness of
society as a whole he saw as necessary if the social and economic
costs of dependency in the twentieth century were to be equitably
shared. REA lowered the minimum age for pension plan participants
from twenty-five to twenty-one, established provisions for automatic
survivor benefits and required that plans obey domestic relations
court orders in cases of divorce.

Many of the objectives for social welfare identified by
Titmuss have been mandated by REA. Congress, as a contingency for
preferential tax treatment of these corporate income security plans,

has forced this traditionally male-oriented private "enclave" to
recognize and accept the lifetime career patterns of women. In addition, REA addresses the special needs of spouses as economic partners
of employees.

REA and the Corporations

The informants for this study did not take kindly to REA.
The administrative changes imposed upon the employers were burdensome
and expensive. REA required a rather radical change in the frame of
reference of many of the study participants if the economic and social
value of the act was to be perceived. These decision makers used the
usual "economic efficiency" yardstick where the focus was on the value
of the dollar in the present to measure the benefit of REA to the
beneficiaries, and found it wanting.

There was little recognition among the compensation managers
as a group that REA was designed to socialize the market, as well as
financially redress institutionalized discrimination against women
employees, and against marriage as an economic unit. Specifically, REA
standards are intended to overcome the discrimination experienced by
women and spouses through the corporate pension plans. According to
Olympia Snowe, the Congresswoman from Maine, the passage of REA

was a necessary step in the fight to eliminate all barriers
to full equality for women . . . to a large extent their poverty
[women's] can be attributed to the failure of retirement income
policies to recognize the economic value of the work women do in
the home and the unique cycles of women and children.

Congress explained that, "The Retirement Equity Act requires greater equity under private pension plans between workers, between spouses and between the workplace and dependents" (U.S. Congress, House, Committee on Ways and Means, 1984, p. 14).

These corporations must now give credits toward pension benefits for employee absence due to pregnancy, newborne care and child adoption. REA also assures prompt benefits payments to eligible employees, restricts exclusion from plans for reasons of advanced age and protects benefits of rehired employees. It is significant that "credited" service rather than concurrent service with the corporation is the new measure for determining vested benefits under qualified plans. All service performed after age eighteen must be counted when calculating the vested portion of a worker's benefit; that is, the years of service before a "break-in-service" must be counted toward retirement unless the number of one-year breaks is five or more. This clause is directed specifically to the employee who wishes to have children.

REA also made significant changes which now protect the interests of spouses and the survivors of employees. To protect vested benefits both the spouse and the employee are required to sign waivers in the presence of a notary if benefits are to be distributed to someone other than the spouse. Belatedly, now spouses of employees who die before retirement are eligible for employee benefits at the intended time of retirement.

REA also recognized the increase in multiple marriages. Divorced spouses can now have both employer death benefits and retirement assets protected through a "qualified domestic relations order" recommended by the courts. REA also increases the dollar limit for qualified retirement plans that provides for immediate lump-sum distribution of pension benefits of an employee who dies or terminates employment before "normal" retirement age. REA raised the limit from $1,750 to $3,500. In an effort to guarantee complete information for employees, Congress requires the corporate plan administrators to inform the pension plan participant of the applicable tax advantages available to the beneficiary who takes a lump-sum distribution. To discourage the pension trust fund fiduciaries from protecting the investment portfolio at the expense of the employee, a five thousand dollar fine is imposed by the IRS if participants are not notified.

Only Rux at Pillsbury had a positive comment about REA. He called it an "administrative hassle," but "the right thing to do." Shebick at Super Valu called it "sham as far as women are concerned, benefits in absolute dollars will be nothing." He quite correctly pointed out that pensions that are designed to support a thirty-year career average and pay benefits in relation to the average pay of the last five years will pay benefits in the early years which are meaningless. Missed were the social implications of REA for the now androgynous employee population and the family unit. Shebick was equally as critical of the pre-retirement survivors benefits which he characterized as an "administrative dog" and minimized the value of this requirement to surviving spouses. He based his opinion on the fact that the economic benefit would not be available to the beneficiary until the employee-participant's normal age of retirement. He saw this lag in time for the delivery of the benefit as a factor which severely limited the cost efficiency of the benefit. He again quite correctly explained that plans which are terminated cease to grow under the same invest-ment conditions as current plans. When questioned about the value of the dollars if they were taken in a lump sum and reinvested, his response was, "They won't do that, they'll spend it."

On the other hand, the informant from 3M agreed that REA was an administrative headache, but said the 3M already had many of the features in place and only needed to make some administrative changes. Schutte did suggest that REA might go a long way in discouraging defined benefit plans in these corporations. Defined contribution plans, by their nature, escape much of the administrative red tape of REA as well as the corporate costs for PBGC premiums which auto-matically increase with the legislated decrease in the age of pension plan participation from age twenty-five to twenty-one.

> I think recent legislation went too far. It has gotten too
> political. Almost as though we are going through in private
> pensions now, what we went through in Social Security in the
> 1960s and 1970s, when we tried to do so much to cover so many
> tiny situations that it became a real burden administratively
> and also very costly.

Discussing the administrative costs of REA, the 3M informant pointed out that the challenge to administrative change is greatly reduced in large and technologically sophisticated corporations such

as those studied here. Schutte discussed the system for employee
record keeping at 3M:

> We have a record for everyone who works here that goes back to
> 1963 which we can pull out with the greatest of ease. It would
> take hundreds of people [without computers] . . . our payroll
> department has either remained the same, over the years, or even
> cut back.

One of the difficulties REA poses to the corporation is the
response to multiple marriages among employees. Changes in spouses of
employees is not a variable that has been an accepted matter of the
employee's record in the past. The informant at 3M commented that the
"divorce papers were already coming in," as a result of REA. This
situation is likely to get worse before it gets better.

At Honeywell, the complaint focused on the "spousal consent"
clause, which requires the spouse to approve distribution of retirement benefits to someone other than themselves. The informant did not
see this new rule as inappropriate. Rather, his complaint was that
his office often found it difficult or impossible to negotiate a
consensus between couples and then get the job done! This negotiation
of interpersonal issues among employees, especially key personnel, was
considered to be outside the role that should be expected of the
employer.

Hamacher at Dayton Hudson called REA a "son of a gun" and
said, "I know who made out on that one--the file cabinet industry and
the paper business." He further complained that it reflected "a lack
of sophistication [by Congress] of the real world situation," alluding
as did the informant from Honeywell, to the personal and business

relationships of key employees to their spouses. Hamacher, echoing

the informant at 3M, also suggested that it would encourage corpora-

tions to shift their emphasis from defined benefit plans to defined

contribution plans.

> We wouldn't have all that crap--it would be simple, because
> it's all individually accounted for--so these divorce cases--
> spreading a pension is very difficult, whereas defined contri-
> butions, $10,000 in the account, it's easy, five and five. And
> adding death benefits under REA I think is stupid--we could have
> then cut our life insurance benefits back--we didn't do that--
> but I like to have each plan do what it is supposed to do--
> retirement plan should pay for retirement, get death benefits
> out of there, get disability out of there--get all that crap
> out of there.

Hamacher mirrors the frame of reference of other informants.

At Pillsbury, where the attitude about the philosophy behind REA was

positive, the informant disagreed that death benefits should be a

special entitlement. In his words, "A pension is not an estate, we

have life insurance for that. A pension is a pension for the

employee." REA has forced compensation managers to reconceptualize

the traditional relationship of employee benefits for retirement to

the economic well-being of the family unit as a whole.

At General Mills, Richie took Congress to task as did other

informants, saying

> The scary part . . . they don't know what the hell they're
> doing. They're numb . . . they're experimenting right now. The
> real issue for us is whether or not we get put at a competitive
> disadvantage. Benefit legislation is going to do very little to
> severely impact basic business at General Mills.

Schutte agrees that at 3M the decision to "pension or not--is controlled in reality by our competitive position." The competitive position in this case refers to the ability of the corporation to attract and retain key employees.

The New Question for the Corporation

All these large corporations have income security plans for retirement that are based on similar assumptions about the needs of employees. All the plans in these corporations follow a similar pattern, and all are subject to ERISA standards. Differences reflect slight variations in the demographics of the employed population. These similarities suggest that no one company will have a significant advantage or disadvantage on this score.

With the limits placed on tax advantages for key employees, Congress has become the "great equalizer." The question has changed for these compensation professionals in large corporations since the elimination of tax-free funded welfare plans and tax shelters for the discretionary income of key employees. Now the question seems to be: Who among these decision makers can come up with a creative, cost efficient, and socially effective income security plan that recognizes the changing demographics of the workforce and the economic partnership of marriage? In doing this, the corporation must maintain solidarity among all employees, while at the same time attract the key employees necessary to the future growth of the corporation.

Occupational Welfare

Titmuss pointed out that social welfare expenditures should not be analyzed in terms of dollars in and dollars out. Rather, distribution should be evaluated by whether or not it makes a positive contribution to the national income and the national welfare.

Historically, Congressional rhetroic has implied a national attempt on the part of Congress to increase the employer's participation in qualified pension plans. If this rhetoric has substance, then one must wonder why Congress has timed the imposition of both burdensome and costly, as well as psychologically unpopular, changes of REA just when the growth of qualified benefit plans has stagnated. Rhetoric aside, it seems quite likely that the Congressional intent is to discourage rather than encourage the expansion of pension plans among corporate employers.

All the informants in this study that offered defined benefit plans were extremely frustrated with what they felt was overregulation. Not only did the informants feel overregulated, but the rate and the number of changes that have been legislated has led to exasperation and a lack of confidence in the wisdom of Congress. In addition, the actions taken by Congress were frequently seen as unfair, particularly since all these corporations perceive themselves as socially responsible employers.

The corporate decision makers were quite exasperated with Congressional expectations. TEFRA, DEFRA and REA each require significant structural changes in retirement income security plans.

These major social purpose acts covered little more than a
twenty-four month period. Experience since then with the Consolidated
Omnibus Budget Reduction Act (COBRA) (P.L. 99-272), affecting employer
health and welfare plans in 1986, plus knowledge that the Tax Reform
Act was only months away from the completion of this study, did
nothing to lessen the informants' frustration.

The seemingly limitless corporate capacity to assimilate all
the legislated changes in employee benefits plans are a credit to the
efficiency of these organizations. However, the corporate patience is
being tested. The perceived administrative difficulties and costs
involved in complying with new legislation coupled with a perception
that the legislation has failed to improve in any significant way the
economic situation of women, are straws that seem to be bending the
camel's back. The six decision makers that offered defined benefit
plans as the primary means of protecting retirement income are now
questioning the "efficiency" of those plans, some seriously, and some
not as seriously, depending on the demographics of the employee group.
More important to these large corporations than the complexity of new
regulations, the differences in social values, and the expectation of
rising PBGC costs, is the loss of the traditional tax shelters
for personal income perquisites that reward key employees.

Congressional Intent

This investigator suggests that the evidence points to the
Congressional intent to encourage savings and defined contribution
plans and to discourage further development of pension plans. The

1978 Revenue Act set a precedent by offering employees a tax incentive to save, and followed on the heels of the important study done by Munnell (1974). This study identified the employee's psychological dependence on Social Security which had led to a change of savings habits in America. This, coupled with the changing demographics of the population and a longer life expectancy was seen as a social combination with serious implications for the future of the income security of the growing number of the nation's elderly.

A healthy system of pensions for retirement cannot exist within a welfare state unless the nation has adequate savings. Pension plan growth has stagnated which worries Congress because of the welfare state's dependence on the participation of the private sector in meeting income security goals for the aged. However, there are three legs to the income security stool. A focus on the private sector pay-as-you-go savings plans better suits the Congressional goal at this time. The development of private pensions and the increase in pension trust funds will not develop the broad-based capital formation that Congress envisions. In addition, when Congress created the PBGC the extremely high cost to the government of guaranteeing private pension benefits was quite underestimated. Congress needs a graceful way out of this costly obligation.

Aside from the Congressional obligations to pension beneficiaries through the PBGC and the need for capital formation, the utility of pension plans as they are structured at this time is being questioned. The demographics of the work force is now young, more mobile and increasingly female. When qualified defined benefit plans were first developed the workforce was older, less mobile and predominately male.

Congress may have overplayed the hand, however, if the goal is to increase private pension plans. The first task of the deferred compensation executives, seldom articulated, has traditionally been to attract and retain needed key employees with retirement benefits designed around tax shelters. TEFRA has significantly undermined the value of the benefits to these employees in a way that is out of the employer's hands. It is not a matter of corporate cost, but rather one of a statutory tax shelter for the key employees' discretionary income to relieve the tax bite of a high income tax bracket. Coupled with this, Congress put limits on the other favored benefit for these employees with the passage of DEFRA. Congress added the previously tax favored funded welfare benefits for key employees to the tax sheltered chopping block.

If Congressional intent is to encourage defined contribution plans then undermining the utility of pension benefits, threatening the funding mechanisms and forcing changes in the corporate social values may just have that effect.

Congress and the Corporation

If there is any question as to whether or not tax acts are in fact social purpose acts, as Titmuss suggests, the legislation between 1975 and 1985 should have put the question to rest. Titmuss defines welfare as a "complex image or idea held by collective

society." "ERISA compliance" standards reflect the Congressional
recognition of the complexities of collective welfare in a market
economy and the use of differentiated means to attain the welfare goal
of income protection of retirees.

Occupational Welfare

ERISA, the statutory foundation of private income security
plans clearly had social goals. Before ERISA, according to a key
informant, "It wasn't unusual to see retirement plans where people had
to be thirty or thirty-five to participate, and then had to have
twenty years of service before their pension benefits were even
vested."

The informant from Honeywell expressed the changes made by
ERISA standards in the corporation this way, "With federal rules
governing so much of this and corporations responding to societal
needs and to the individual employee's wishes . . . we're not in lock-
step, but we are certainly going in the same direction."

Titmuss has suggested that welfare can be identified by its
function of ameliorating the social costs that exist in the complex
and changing society of the welfare state. Prior to ERISA the rights
of employee participants in private pension plans had no statutory
protection.

The ERISA standards that govern retirement income security
plans now suggest that "contingency welfare" represents a new rela-
tionship--that of the employer to Congress, rather than that of
employee to employer. The power differential in this new arrangement

between employers and Congress is certainly more equitable than that
which existed prior to ERISA between employee and the employer.

Contingencies

Congress has "bribed" the private sector employers with
foregone tax dollars and employee tax shelters to develop income
security plans for both pre and post retirees. These bribes, in the
form of special tax treatment, can be defined as "social welfare."
The dollars used to tempt employers come from the public purse,
serve a social purpose and are contingent upon the employer's strict
compliance with statutory policy.

The participation of employers in this parternship with
Congress has also introduced a link to institutional welfare that has
been missing in the past. The eligibility for, and the distribution
of, tax-supported economic benefits of private income security plans
are now subject, by statute, to both pre and post work oversight by
the IRS. Sponsoring employers can now be held accountable for occupational social welfare systems.

This rather stormy partnership between Congress and the
employers has helped build a three-legged stool for income security
through Social Security, Supplemental Security Insurance, pension
benefits and, more recently, individual employee savings. The "price"
the employer pays for the tax dollars that support these employee
perquisites is compliance to egalitarian ideals. As a result of acts
of Congress, employers in these corporations are being deliberately

socialized to the concept of equity and equality in the distribution of the corporate economic and social resources.

If the immediate needs of the nation have forced Congress to temporarily reassess its preference for pension plans for the economic security of retirees, what better time than now, when the growth of pensions has stagnated, to impose an overwhelming number of rules and regulations to democratize the private sector income security system? Employers defecting from the pension plans in favor of defined contribution and savings plans would serve the national interest of capital formation and the Congressional interest in broadening the tax base. Those employers who remain loyal to the concept of pension plans, at least as a secondary source of income protection, will be modelling new values and becoming socialized to egalitarian ideals. From this dual perspective, it seems that Congress cannot lose.

Employers who participated in this study are still philosophically tied to the concept of a guaranteed income for employees in retirement. The concept, if not the practice, of a thirty-year career is also alive and well at all but Pillsbury among the large corporations. More significant, each of the corporations studied had pension trusts which were over-funded. This means that the costs of corporate pension plans are covered entirely by the earnings of the pension trust. To this can be added the corporate advantage of a tax deduction in the present, which represents real dollars, for a future obligation which, in fact, will cost these corporations nothing in real dollars.

Those are considered high stakes by the informants of this study. Financial advantages, for both the employer and the employee, are considered compelling reasons for retaining pension plans as the primary focus for retirement income security among these corporate sponsors. If qualified defined benefit plans are retained as the primary corporate response to the retiree's economic needs for the above reasons, then the corporate price tag is compliace with ERISA standards. These standards assure an increasingly egalitarian distribution of tax favored retirement benefits within the corporation.

CHAPTER V

INCOME SECURITY PLANS IN THE CORPORATION

The tax incentives available to these corporations for the development of retirement income plans represents a significant source of funding. The plans these employers offer their employees can be considered a manifestation of the corporation's response to the acts of Congress which encourage employers to sponsor income security plans.

This discussion will focus on the provisions these corporations have made for their retirees and the implications of these choices for employees. Plans came in two major categories: (a) defined benefit or pension plans and (b) defined contribution or profit-sharing plans. A third category, the "floor" plan, combines the protection offered by the defined benefit plan and the opportunity offered by the defined contribution plan, and appears to be a harbinger of change.

The Defined Benefit Plan

The large established corporations, Dayton Hudson, General Mills, Honeywell, 3M, Pillsbury and Super Valu, all offer the qualified defined benefit plan (or pension) as their primary vehicle for income protection in retirement. The pension plans were designed to encourage tenure with the corporations and to attract key personnel to the organizations.

154

If each of these corporations is viewed as a microcosm, then the qualified defined pension plans offers employees of the six large corporations what might be seen as a "universal" benefit. Participation is automatic for all employees and can be considered a status right and an entitlement. In each case, the employers take full responsibility for both planning and financing the income protection of the corporate retirees. The corporations assume the economic risks that are involved in meeting the employer's contracted and future obligation. The benefit is "defined" so that the employee can anticipate the dollar amount of the benefit at retirement.

The ability of the corporate pension plan assets to target each individual in the corporation according to his/her individual retirement needs qualifies the pension approach to income protection as cost effective. Pension plans also seem to meet the criteria for social effectiveness by treating employees of the corporation as equal members of a group.

However, what you see is not what you get. Some of these corporations offer pension plans which are based on outdated social and economic assumptions that focus on longevity of service and single career options. For instance, Dayton Hudson offers a pension based on a thirty-year career but the average length of employment is 2.5 years! While at 3M the average length of employment was ten years, this still implies that many employees never attain full employment benefits.

Defined benefit plans also fail to offer protection against inflation for those who are already retired nor does a pension plan protect those who choose to change employers and find their benefits fixed at their date of termination from the corporation. The tenure clause in all pension plans does not adequately reward the new mobile worker and the increasingly female workforce. Women, who still have shorter employment histories than men, now make up fifty-two percent of the full-time workforce (Letter from A. Stanland, U.S. Congress, "Women in America, A Statistical Profile, September 1987). Table 3 shows the economic value of pension earned depends mostly on age.

Vesting

Social allocation in pension plans is further exacerbated by corporate vesting schedules, that is, the time table for employee eligibility for benefits. These policies were originally designed to encourage the retention of employees. In a mobile society, vesting schedules have served to deny more than fifty percent of all newly hired employees any pension benefits because they leave the corporation before vesting occurs (Wall Street Journal, June 5, 1985, p. 36).

Those employees who are vested but choose not to stay with the employer for thirty years are also denied an adequate return on their deferred compensation. Benefits which are vested when the employee leaves the corporation become fixed within the pension trust fund. The younger the employee, then, the greater the erosion of the benefit by inflation. The thirty-five year old employee who leaves the corporation with a seven-year vested pension must wait until age

TABLE 3

ECONOMIC VALUE OF PENSION BENEFIT EARNED BY AGE AND SERVICE

Years of Service	Age						
	35	40	45	50	55	60	65
10	$ 1,500	$ 3,000	$ 5,000	$ 7,000	$21,000	$30,000	$30,000
15	2,000	4,000	6,000	11,000	31,000	44,000	44,000
20		4,000	7,000[a]	13,000	40,000[b]	59,000	59,000
25			8,000	14,000	50,000	73,000	74,000
30				15,000	59,000	87,000	89,000

SOURCE: Courtesy of Pillsbury Corporation, 1986.
NOTE: Two individuals with same final pay ($30,000) and same years of service (20) have earned benefits as follows:

[a]Person A: Hired at age 25, benefit worth $ 7,000 ($ 350/year).
[b]Person B: Hired at age 35, benefit worth $40,000 ($2,000/year).

Economic value of pension earned depends more on age hired than any other factor.

sixty-five to collect benefits. In an economy that has a five percent inflation rate, the benefit will be reduced in value by seventy-five percent before payments begin.

Since the corporate returns on pension trust fund investments tend to rise with inflation, the employee's fixed-dollar pension can be funded by the company at a progressively lower cost as the investments benefit from inflation. The purchasing power of the benefit which is lost to the employee begins to grow in the corporation's pension trust. Hence, the employee's loss is the employer's gain. Vesting, the assurance that benefits are nonforfeitable, tends to give a misleading expectation of income protection for retirement years to the employee who has had more than one employer. The concept of requiring a vesting schedule for employees to become eligible for benefits is inconsistent with the accepted concept of pension benefits as a "foregone increase in wages" or "deferred compensation."

Dayton Hudson, Super Valu and Honeywell have ten-year cliff vesting based on a thirty-year employment career. The employee would be eligible for fifty percent of the accrued pension benefits after five years and one hundred percent after ten years. The catch for many employees is the "thirty-year career" clause. Benefits are based on the actuarially determined average expected income of thirty years of service, and then prorated on actual years served. Since the last years will, in most cases, be the highest paid, any employee who separates from the corporation before a tenure of twenty-five years suffers a significant penalty. General Mills, 3M and Pillsbury all

have a five-year vesting schedule. Whether vesting is on a five-year
or a ten-year schedule, the participants accrued benefits are severely
reduced by early departure.

The immediate vesting of all pension benefits, recognized by
compensation professionals as "deferred wages" would seem to be appropriate. Pension financing facts support the validity of the sugges-
tion. Over a thirty-year period pension benefits, or deferred wages,
cost the employer about one-eighth of the cost of immediate wages
(Wall Street Journal, June 5, 1985, p. 36). This is a high premium
for the employee to pay for automatic contributions to an employer's
promise of income during retirement.

Although all the informants did agree that the benefit obligation paid into the trust on behalf of the employee could be
considered an entitlement, and also deferred wages, they did not agree
on the subject of vesting (see Honeywell letter in Appendix C). At
Pillsbury, Rux "was absolutely in favor" of proposed legislation to
reduce allowable vesting to five years. He estimated that such a
change would increase plan costs to the corporation by ten to twenty
percent because of their younger, mobile work force but found it "in
line with the young and female workforce." Schutte at 3M said that it
would increase administration costs and not increase benefits propor-
tionately because "the plan was set up for the final years."

The 1986 Tax Reform Act (TRACT) passed since the completion of
this study has mandated shorter vesting schedules for qualified
benefit plans. This change upsets the previous balance achieved by

corporate finances of cost effectiveness and social effectiveness of pension plans in these corporations. This change also upsets the investment patterns of the pension trust fund.

Anticipating the changes of TRACT, the informant from Dayton Hudson saw the changes as inconsistent with the corporate goal of employee retention and reward through pension benefits. In his opinion, any reduction in present rules would substitute the concept of "vesting" for one of "termination pay."

A termination approach to the accrued pension benefits of the employee who separates from the company is an interesting concept which would seem to benefit the mobile employee who is also often young and often not financially secure. Termination pay, as opposed to a vested benefit, would change the locus of control to those funds from employer to employee and give the employee the choice regarding future investment of the funds. The employee concerned about retirement could invest the benefit and thus capitalize on the short-term employment experience, rather than lose what has accrued to benefits. Currently, this vested employee has no choice but to suffer the consequences of "fixed benefits" in the former employee's pension trust fund.

Of course, the danger here is the employee who is more concerned with the present circumstances for good, or not so good, reasons. If the employee's choice is to spent the termination pay, then there would be no investment in retirement income security.

Risk

The security implied by defined pension plans seems more
illusion than real. This concept has been eroded by a now more mobile
workforce, the termination or early retirement from employment because
of skill obsolescence, the changing demographics of the population,
and an economy subject to inflation. Further, in today's rapidly
changing world there is no guarantee that corporations will still be
economically viable in thirty years' time.

For companies that default on their pension obligations, the
protection offered employees by the Pension Benefit Guarantee
Corporation (PBGC) only insures obligations to the date of termination
of the plan. In addition, the PBGC only insures a percentage of the
vested benefits. For the employees of successful and socially responsible corporations, such as those studied here, there is always the
risk of an unfriendly take-over which often results in structural
changes. The new employers are under no obligation to continue the
pension plan. Pension benefits that are terminated for any reason
become fixed for the employee at that date and so will not fulfill the
retirement income security promised by the previous employer.

The term participation in a pension plan is not synonymous with
the term beneficiary. When national statistics tout the high percentage of participation by corporations in private income security
plans, those statistics address participation of employees in these
plans but not the employee's eligibility or the adequacy of those
benefits, which are the more crucial questions.

The Defined Contribution Plan

All the corporations, both large and small, offered their employees defined contribution plans. This includes those corporations which also offer pension plans to their employees. Defined contribution plans are said to give employees the opportunity to share directly in the success of the company. In this way the employee can impact his/her future benefits through effective work performance and also develop a sense of belonging to the corporation. Profit sharing plans are said by these decision makers to enhance the partnership between employer and employee, encourage teamwork and productivity and, all the while, recognize the worth of the individual employee.

The income protection offered through these plans depends on the amount the employee can contribute to the plan, the amount the employer agrees to contribute and the level of the success of the investment strategy. The employee is promised no predetermined retirement benefit for the post work years. Each employee has an individual account with the corporation and, if the employee chooses to leave the company, the full amount of his/her contributions are available to him/her. In most cases the employer's share is available on a schedule of less than five years. At the far end, the 3M contribution is available at five years while the Cray Research contribution is available immediately. At Cray Research, one might say that the concept of retirement income as "deferred wages" is made manifest with the absence of a vesting schedule for the employer contributions.

Unlike pension plans, the defined contribution plans are fully funded annually on a pay-as-you-go basis. The employee avoids the risks associated with underfunded pension plans, unfriendly take-overs or corporate failure. By law, the employee's contribution to the plan is immediately vested in a personal account.

It is worth noting that the defined contribution plan which has been designed by the sponsor to net the same retirement benefit as a defined benefit plan will pay out more in benefits to the employee who separates from the company before normal retirement age. Hence the defined contribution plan seems to better serve the young and mobile workers, and early retirement trends.

Also, the defined contribution plans offered by these corporations allow the dependents of deceased employees to collect benefits at the time of death rather than at what would have been the employee's "normal" retirement age, as with the pension plans (Moreen, 1985). This serves the survivors' immediate economic and social needs of the family rather than the future retirement needs of the individual.

Resources made available during a crisis might help the survivor structure a financial plan in the present which will be economically viable in the future. Such a plan would be likely to generate income protection for retirement. Defined contribution plans tend to broaden the concept of income security to include the employee's life span rather than limiting the concept to the retirement years.

Risk

The informants discussed the disadvantages of the defined
contribution plans of which employees and policy proponents need to be
aware. In the years when profits are down, the corporation will contribute little or maybe nothing to the defined contribution plan. In
addition, employees bear the financial burden of poor investments made
by the trust, as well as the vagaries of the financial market. A
depreciation in the financial market can quickly offset gains from
company contributions to the plan. The employee has little control
over anything except his/her own financial contribution.

In contrast to the defined benefit plans, the employee is not
guaranteed a certain income on retirement. Employer contributions
depend on the economic circumstances of the employer as well as the
largess of each employing organization. In this study, corporate
contributions ranged from seven percent of salary to eleven percent of
salary if the defined contribution plan was the primary vehicle for
income protection in retirement. In those corporations where the
defined contribution plan played a supplemental role, the contributions
ranged from zero to six percent of the salary. The amount of the
corporate contribution, in each case, was determined annually by the
board of directors, based on the past year's profits and next year's
corporate expectations.

There are advantages for the younger mobile employee in having
a defined contribution plan as opposed to a defined benefit plan.
However, if the plan has been in effect only a short time, or if the

employee is both new and older, then the plan discriminates against the older employee whose retirement is more imminent. This then becomes a more serious social issue in terms of the income protection of the corporation's retirees.

The weaknesses of a defined contribution plan can be particularly critical if an established corporation such as Dayton Hudson experiences a take-over and the retirement income security plans, now predominately defined benefit plans, are terminated in favor of defined contribution plans. Those employees whose benefits had been actuarially determined based on the average income of the last five or ten years would be caught short in retirement without a supplemental plan to make up the shortfall. The employee's benefits would become fixed as of the date of the change.

For participants in defined contribution plans, there is protection from inflation. The most common form of benefit at retirement is a lump-sum distribution which cannot, obviously, be adjusted for the cost of living as could a pension benefit which is still within the control of the corporation. Pensions also provide some inflation protection if they are based on the final average salary of an employee.

Retirement based on a defined contribution plan can be a little like Russian roulette. The benefit received depends on the market value of the participant's account on the day the benefit is determined. The present unpredictability of the stock market gives some indication of the unknowns which face the employee who is

depending on a defined contribution plan for retirement income. The
situation is critical and the consequences irreversible for the
retiree whose benefit is determined during a period when the financial
market dictates low equity prices and/or depressed bond prices.

The only control that an employee can exercise over this
situation is to choose the date of retirement with care. In other
words, those who play Russian roulette should not pull the trigger and
retire if they think there is a bullet in the chamber that will kill
them!

The Measure of Economic Need in Retirement

Contributions to the retirement plan by the employer are based
on the wages of the employee. This represents the Titmuss criticism
of occupational welfare as "contingency welfare." The adequacy of the
employer contribution is determined by the status and the merit of the
employee within the corporation rather than on the employee's
perceived income needs alone.

To compound the problem of employer contributions based on
wages, the contributions of the employee to future income security is
also based on the same measure. For the low-waged that is double
jeopardy. Thus, the employee's ability to build an economically
secure future is restricted. The first restriction is the statutory
limits on employer and employee contributions to a deferred compensation account based on wages and the second restriction is the discretionary income available to each individual employee. The corporate

employee with the least discretionary income will experience the most economic and social discrimination in building income security for retirement.

Employee Preference

All the informants reported that employees expressed a preference for qualified defined contribution plans. At Honeywell, the informant "wondered if employees knew what was happening." When employees seem to have a preference for participatory plans care must be taken to separate what is a psychological preference of the modern employee for choice and autonomy in planning for the future and what is illusion in terms of hard economic facts which will have direct bearing on the employee's future income security. The economic facts are based on many variables. The most important are the element of risk incurred by the employee, the profitability of the corporation, the trust investment strategy, the age of the employee and the amount of discretionary income available to the individual.

Income Security in the Smaller Corporation

The small companies--Wilcox Paper, Toro and Cray Research-- were able to design qualified defined contribution plans that closely reflected the demographics of their companies. When asked by the investigator how important it was to design income security plans based on the make-up of the employees, Bartolett at Toro said, "Anyone with an ounce of smarts recognizes that the retirement program is an integral part of your employment package."

Wilcox Paper

At Wilcox Paper there are forty employees who are all white, predominately male and between the ages of thirty-five and seventy. Because the company employs fewer than one hundred employees, it escapes the detailed ERISA standards. However, the corporation must convince the IRS that the plan is "reasonable" in order to qualify for the special tax treatment.

The profit-sharing plan has been in place at Wilcox Paper since 1975 when the company was at risk financially and not in a position to assume the future obligations of a pension plan. This plan, designed to generate business for the company as well as to build income security for the employees, is based on a psychology of employee incentive. In an all-or-nothing approach, the company promised a fifteen percent profit-share the first year. Now the policy is a guarantee of eleven to fifteen percent of profits annually for all salaried employees and a guaranteed rate of interest on investments of eleven to fifteen percent annually. According to Dick Mast, "The company writes one hundred percent of the cost off as expense." There is no withdrawal unless the employee leaves the company and there is no loan feature. But the company offers its employees interest-free loans "with no strings attached" in cases of hardship on an informal basis. This type of loan has been sanctioned by the IRS since the Economic Recovery Tax Act and is used in the large corporations for upper-level executives. The employee is offered a choice on retirement of lump-sum distribution or gradual

withdrawal. Since 1975, only three employees have retired. One left
the funds with the company investments and two took lump-sum
distributions.

Only at Wilcox Paper are employees formally involved in
profit-share decisions. A committee made up of the CEO, a board
member and a salesperson are responsible for reviewing the plan. In
describing the plan to the investigator, the CEO demonstrated how an
employee making thirty thousand dollars annually (what he considered
a starting salary, based on commissions), working twenty-five years
for the company and averaging the same percentage of profit-sharing
experienced by the company in the last ten years, would retire with
$250,000 in deferred income These funds, with an expected minimum
interest potential of ten percent, can be expected to yield an annual
retirement income of twenty-five thousand dollars, not considering
Social Security benefits. Those who averaged forty thousand dollars
per year could expect one-half million dollars in deferred compensation, without Social Security benefits. The integration of pension
plans with Social Security, practiced in all the large corporations,
inhibits the over-pensioning possible at Wilcox, by actuarially establishing a retirement income which only replaces fifty to seventy
percent of pre-retirement income. Over-pensioning can be considered a
"cost" to the taxpayer because it is generated by special tax treatment. Over-pensioning is not possible when the public and the
private plans are integrated.

Toro

      Toro has had a profit-share income security plan for retirees
since 1952. The company prides itself on meeting the needs of the
"people who make up the company." Bartolett feels the importance of
considering corporate demographics as " . . . when put on a scale of
one to ten, that's eleven." The defined contribution plan at Toro has
no withdrawal clause while the participant is employed at Toro, but
enjoys a short two-year vesting schedule for corporate contributions
which gives the plan a high level of portability.

      At Toro, retirement income security is designed around
Employee Stock Options Plans (ESOPs), a profit-share vehicle encouraged by Congress with special tax treatment. Bartolett demonstrated
that an employee earning thirty thousand dollars per year, under past
circumstances, based on a thirty-year career at Toro, could expect to
accrue ninety thousand dollars at retirement. The investment of this
capital at retirement age, at a projected minimum of ten percent,
would give the employee an income of nine thousand dollars plus the
Social Security benefits.

      The 401(k) at Toro is considered a pre-tax retirement savings
device for employees that will enrich the retirement benefits to the
company plan. According to this informant, the company developed the
vehicle at little cost to give employees the best opportunity possible
to invest collectively in their future. The 401(k) benefits which
accrue are not a part of the final estimated retirement loan feature.
Bartolett reported that at Toro the 401(k) employee participation rate

had increased every year. He saw this plan as "one of the most
popular benefit devices we've ever had." His explanation for the
popularity of the plan was that "every employee, whether he admits it
or not, has a concern for their future."

Cray Research

The Cray Research plan is designed to meet the needs of the
young mobile computer industry employees and represents the third time
the plan has been redesigned in eleven years. The future at Cray
Research is considered uncertain and portability of benefits (the
ability of an employee to cash in and roll over investment in the
company when separating) is seen as an important feature of this
deferred compensation plan. Cray's new plan has three parts. The
first is a deferred profit sharing piece based on about four percent
of expected earnings. This is considered the first obligation of the
plan. The second part of the plan is employee investment savings
based on the 401(k). At Cray Research employees are allowed to
contribute fifteen percent of pay. This contribution is supplemented
by a company contribution of fifty cents on the dollar for the first
two thousand dollars of the employee contribution. The third piece of
the plan is distributed profit-sharing, that is, an annual cash
"bonus", projected to be ten percent of eligible compensation.

> We restructured the whole thing and utilized the 401(k) plan--
> it's a beautiful plan, it's really working well--we have about
> seventy percent of the employees that are participating at some
> level in the plan. We're hoping that the tax changes that are
> just around the corner won't impact the plan too much. It will
> lower the maximum contribution that employees can make, we know
> that for sure. . . . .

When Cray Research restructured their defined contribution plan, the concept of "Life After Cray" became integral to the philosophy of the plan. Cray does not expect or encourage employee longevity because of rapid change in general and the uncertainty in the computer industry in particular. Profit-sharing to make employees financially independent, together with education in alternate career choices to defang skill obsolescence, are expected to encourage career change for those who want to and for those who must. Johnson illustrated the need and wisdom of such a plan when he described the not-so-gradual and continuing replacement of semi-skilled employees with robots in the supercomputer manufacturing plant in Wisconsin. A supplemental defined benefit plan, or "floor plan", was considered for this population during restructuring of the plan but was not adopted.

Discussion

These decision makers in the smaller corporations focus on defined contribution plans and suggest that they offer employees a promise of opportunity in the present rather than the promise of security in the future. The portable profit-share plans reported here can be conceptualized as offering "income security" without the qualification of "retirement". In a mobile changing society income security that is flexible enough to use in a crisis, or portable to a new employment location, can open doors to opportunity and mitigate a crisis during the working years. On the other hand, the flexibility of the plan can leave the mobile spendthrift employee without adequate income security in the retirement years.

Toro: A Special Case

Toro represents a special case among the corporations studied. The corporate plan for income security in retirement is unusual in that the defined contribution plan at Toro is "protected" by a pension "floor" plan. With this plan, if the profit-share picture at the time of an employee's retirement is such that the target of a sixty percent replacement of pre-retirement income is not reached then the defined benefit plan comes into play to make up the difference. The pension benefit acts as a supplement to the defined contribution plan for those employees who stay with the corporation. This is a reverse of the traditional relationship between defined benefit and defined contribution plans found in the large corporations.

Toro was the only corporation with this model in place. The informant knew of no other corporation in the area that had adopted a similar plan. Floor plans are discussed in the literature and are sometimes called "hybrid" plans (Beam and McFadden, 1985). During the interviews with the informant at Toro, the floor plan designed for lower-waged clerical staff was never mentioned. In fact, Bartolett was less than complementary about corporations that "resorted to pensions," so the evidence of a pension plan at Toro on the IRS form 5500 came as a surprise to the investigator. Inquiry revealed that the informant had not even thought of the floor as part of "the plan" at Toro because it came into play so seldom and was not a significant expense. The 1978 net assets required to meet pension obligations were only $132,850 and even less in 1985 when $119,820 was held in trust to meet expected obligations (from IRS 5500, 1978, 1986).

Toro first considered this adaption to their plan following their experience with the 1972 and 1975 decline in the stock market. As a corporation, Toro was reaching the age in the 1970s where it was beginning to have an increase in the number of retirees. The corporate decision makers did not like what they saw in terms of the protection of the pre-retirement standard of living for some of their employees. Toro found that when both stocks and bonds go down in value together, there is little that employers or employees can do to protect themselves through investments. The situation becomes one of double jeopardy for the employee in a profit-share plan when corporate profits go down as well because this reduces the corporate contribution to the retirement plan.

Following this experience, the corporation dedicated a fixed portion of the corporate retirement assets to company control. A pension trust fund was developed and the supplemental pension plan introduced. This floor plan at Toro requires the company to be in compliance with ERISA standards for pension trust funds. Toro's adoption of the floor plan for their office and clerical staff means the corporation is responsible for annual premiums to the Pension Benefit Guarantee Corporation costs of $8.50 per participant, avoided in the straight profit-sharing plans.

The "efficiency" of the PBGC costs are measured in the large corporation in proportion to the number of beneficiaries in the pension plans. By those standards, Toro's small number of participants and smaller number of beneficiaries for the defined benefit portion of the income security plan makes the relative costs of the PBGC inefficient. One can assume that decision makers at Toro used the concept of adequacy here in preference to "efficiency".

In response to the question of whether or not changing from one type of plan to another might be difficult, Bartolett felt that the key issue was the employee's relationship with the corporation. This company committed a great deal of time initially to communicating the change to employees. He commented that it is necessary to "re-traditionalize them." The task at Toro was made easier by the high level of trust in the company held by its employees.

Discussion

Toro has established a clear example of a well-balanced three-legged stool for income security in retirement. The income protection afforded the retiree through the floor plan assures the beneficiary of a certain level of income protection which secures the private pension leg. The savings leg to the stool is secured by the opportunity offered employees for participation in the 401(k). An opportunity, at Toro, that is completely divorced from the calculation of employee's retirement benefits and will be seen for what it is, the employee's personal savings. The hardship clause of this savings device makes it both popular and appropriate for all age groups. The third leg to balance this stool is, of course, the employee's entitlement to Social Security.

Academically speaking, this clear distinction between what is considered an investment of income and what is savings, found in the Toro plan, is critical to planning effective future income security both at the micro/employee level and the macro/policy level. Drucker (1976, p. 11) points out that investments and savings are not the same, as Keynesian economics have led us to believe. Rather, capital formation, or personal savings, are a pre-requirement of investment for future income security at the national and the individual level. This has implications for employers and employees who are developing income security plans.

Drucker seems to be suggesting that when one has both a cart and a horse it is important to understand how they work together. If the horse and the cart are to be mutually beneficial, it is necessary to put the horse up front; that is, savings and investments are a team rather than synonymous.

The floor plan offers employees both investment opportunity and income security when planning for retirement. The assumption at Toro is that employees are capable of managing their income security in retirement but that unexpected circumstances over which they have no control can jeopardize their plans. The Toro experience supports these assumptions. The pension plan which eliminates the risk of an inadequate income in retirement seldom comes into play. However, in times of financial uncertainty, which no one can seem to accurately

predict, the employee most in need will be protected by the employer's
pension plan.

The basis for the adoption of this plan at Toro might be said
to reflect Titmuss' altruism. The corporate "regard" for the
employees at Toro led to a change in plans with the specific "intent"
of protecting the retiree to "ameliorate the costs of a changing
industrialized society."

The floor plan, which combines the opportunity offered by a
defined contribution plan with the security of a pension plan income,
mirrors the welfare state's model for income protection of the aged.
Social Security, associated with employment opportunities, is the
primary vehicle for income protection. For those who do not attain
the desired minimum level of financial support Supplemental Security
Income, associated with need, comes into play.

The Financing of Income Security Plans

Technically, the question is not HOW these corporations
finance income security plans but rather the question is WHEN do the
corporations finance these plans. Pension plans have long been
attractive to employers because of the ability of the employer to
promise a future benefit to the employee and receive a tax deduction
from profits in the present. In other words, the employer is being
"paid" by the IRS in the present for a future financial obligation to
employees.

The defined contribution plans, on the other hand, required
that the employer meet the financial obligation in the present and the

IRS, in a sense, pays in the present. The advantage of the defined
benefit plans is that employers have been able to generate working
capital by way of what can be called a "tax-free loan" from the IRS.

According to these decision makers the choice between a
defined benefit plan and a defined contribution plan may well depend
on which is in the best financial position, the pension trust or the
corporation. This investigator suggests that this might be a unique
time in the history of these corporations. According to the informants, all the pension trust funds of these corporations are over-
funded at this time. Also, according to the 1985 annual reports, all
these corporations have an excellent profit picture. With both the
corporation and the trust funds doing well, this space in time may be
unique for corporate compensation professionals. Given this situation,
it seems possible that the decision makers will have some elasticity
of choice in the design of their retirement income plans. This could
lead to structural change.

Will the Corporate Financial Strategy Change?

As already noted, the question the corporate decision makers
are asking themselves now is, "When should retirement income benefits
be paid for, when the benefit comes due or should corporations pay-as-
they-go?" The demographics of the workforce, financial position and
corporate philosophy have already dictated the choice to pay-as-you-go
at Wilcox Paper, Toro and Cray Research.

The investigator posed several questions to the respondents to try to determine which way the decision makers were leaning, toward defined benefit plans or toward defined contribution plans. Special attention was paid to those corporations heavily invested in qualified defined benefit plans. These questions were:

1. In your corporation has the role of the qualified contribution plan for retirement changed since 1981?

2. As you have worked in this area, have you seen a shift in where the corporate emphasis has been placed?

3. Does a trade-off between PBGC costs which are associated with pension plans and security for the retiree and employee participation in qualified contribution plans with a feature of unpredictability for the retiree seem acceptable?

4. Will the benefits history and plans of your corporation, and its implied expectations, conflict with the changing social aims and employment patterns of workers? (Questions 19, 31, 43 and 46 of Questionnaire, see Appendix D.)

Corporate Response

1. In your corporation has the role of the qualified contribution plan for retirement changed since 1981?

All the large corporations reported an increased emphasis on defined contribution plans.

Honeywell. "We have projected plans to change the ratio of our emphasis on defined benefit and defined contribution over time [less of the former]."

180

Super Valu. "We're looking at it more seriously, and we've taken a step in that direction with adding the 401(k) plan [1984]."

3M. "Yes, the 401(k) is a great alternative!"

General Mills. "Defined benefit gives you life income. Defined contribution gives you economic opportunity, a different animal."

Pillsbury. "Yes, paternalism [of defined benefit] is a big issue. Trusts do well during inflation, beneficiaries do not . . . the defined contribution has perceptual utility."

Dayton Hudson. "Yes, because I've always felt there was never incentive for people to save money--always incentive for people to spend."

    2. As you have worked in this area, have you seen a shift in where the corporate emphasis has been placed?

All the managers also agreed that the focus of the corporation was shifting toward defined contribution plans.

Honeywell. "Definitely seen a shift at Honeywell toward the 401(k) and other profit-sharing plans."

Toro. "I think pensions are for sick companies."

General Mills. "I think we're on the verge of a shift away from defined benefit to defined contribution."

3. Does a trade-off between PBGC costs which are associated
with pension plans and security for the retiree and employee
participation in qualified contribution plans with a feature of
unpredictability for the retiree seem acceptable?

The answer to this question was less clear.

3M. 3M does not see the PBGC as a "driving force," only a
"maddening" one!

General Mills. Congress is struggling with this "maddening"
issue and has suggested keeping the $8.50 premium and adding a supple-
mental premium of two hundred dollars per participant to those corporations that have underfunded plans.

Some respondents gave details on why the PBGC was "maddening".

Honeywell. Amborn reported that "62,000 defined benefit
participants multiplied by $8.50 translates into about five million
dollars at Honeywell."

Dayton Hudson. Addressing the increase in participation in
defined benefit plans mandated by the Retirement Equity Act, Hamacher
said, "Reducing the age [of participation] to twenty-one didn't bother
me, it cost me nothing in pension benefits--what it cost me was
another $100,000 in PBGC costs because I had to bring in all those
twenty-one to twenty-five year olds.

General Mills. General Mills claimed:

> The intention [of Congress] was to shove liability to the
> private sector because if they didn't it would become the
> liability of the federal government. Put the fox right in with
> the chickens. Through the PBGC they're [Congress] stuck--that
> is a major piece of social policy.

Super Valu. Shebick expressed a generally held attitude among

the plan directors. He considered the concept on which the PBGC was

established to be legitimate but shared that corporations like Super

Valu resent "irresponsible employers dumping underfunded plans on

PBGC, causing rates to go up, causing responsible employers with well-

funded plans, such as ourselves, to in effect subsidize irresponsible

employers."

Pillsbury. Rux added that it "makes more sense to pull out of

the plan."

3M. On the other hand, Schutte said that the PBGC cost would

not be a determining factor in whether or not 3M offered a defined

benefit plan. 3M was also concerned that plan managers were pushing

defined contribution to avoid PBGC premiums, rather than because they

felt it was the best choice for the employee and the corporation.

All the managers approved of the concept of the PBGC and felt

that the system could be modified not to penalize the viable companies.

They would find risk-related premiums acceptable. This would assess

the viable companies less and those at risk more.

It was interesting that all the decision makers reported that

their corporations were placing a new emphasis on the defined contribution plan. Also, it seems that in some cases the defined benefit plans will be playing second fiddle to the defined contribution plan, rather than the other way around. However, all but one of these decision makers felt that the pension plan represented a financially valuable and risk-free benefit whether the employees realized it or not!

4. Will the benefits history of your corporation, and its implied expectations, conflict with the changing social and employment patterns of the employees?

All the managers felt their corporation would change with the demands of the times! Although some did admit that it might not happen overnight!

3M. At 3M, Shutte spoke for the majority when he said that the objectives of 3M's plans were flexible and employee-oriented, and not locked into the past.

General Mills. Richie said, "I think our patterns will change as the patterns of employment change."

Pillsbury. Rux underscored the point for Pillsbury, "I don't think so, plans are designed to reflect the change of social and employment patterns of career folk. Pillsbury is conscious of needs and shifts of career women."

Super Valu. Super Value was less emphatic. "Warehouses have more traditional needs--they're changing--over time--yes."

These corporations, then, are seeing a new role for the defined contribution plan. Also, they have observed a shift in the corporate plan emphasis to defined contribution plans. In addition, they have confidence that their organizations will change with the times. The times seem to indicate the increased regulation of pension plans, an emphasis on defined contribution plans and an employee interest in participation in defined contributions plans.

Dayton Hudson.

> From an employee relations standpoint . . . they [employees] could care less about a pension plan, other than we have one. Our defined contribution plan . . . now they understand that . . . they've got some dollars [invested] . . . we're a touchy-feely society, right? And the 401(k) plan is a touchy-feely kind of thing.

This suggests a move to emphasize pay-as-you-go financing in these corporations. This has implications for both the employer and the employee. A move to pay-as-you-go plans represents a significant change in the funding structure of private income security plans among the large corporations. For employees it means assuming responsibility for future income security that in the past has been assumed by the employer.

Discussion

If all but one of the decision makers is philosophically committed to the value of the defined benefit plan, and they do not find the concept of the PBGC inconsistent, one wonders what has motivated them to consider a new emphasis. This investigator suggests that these corporations are responding first to TEFRA which voided the traditional perquisite used to attract and retain key employees by making those benefits taxable as personal income. Also, TEFRA lowered the level at which private plans could integrate with Social Security thus upsetting the corporate funding patterns. Second, DEFRA established a mechanism for corporations to legally withdraw excess assets from pension trust funds to use as capital. This allows these corporate managers some additional flexibility. On the other hand, DEFRA curtailed the tax advantaged pre-funding tradition for corporate funded welfare plans. In addition, DEFRA restricted tax advantages on corporate contributions that fund benefits to those funds which go to retirees. Third, the Financial Standard Accounting Board is asking hard questions about the "ownership" of the pension trust funds. Corporate decision makers are not sure that the pension trust funds will not be next on the Congressional assault list. Fifth, REA and the attendant rules and regulations have made the simplicity of the pay-as-you-go plans much more attractive to the decision makers.

Taken together, the contingencies now required for corporations to qualify for preferential tax treatment through defined pension plans have made them seem much less attractive to decision makers as an employee benefit. On the other side of the ledger, Congress has made the contingencies for defined contribution and savings plans very attractive to both employers and employees. Pressure is being exerted on the traditional means by which corporations have delivered

occupational benefits. A point worth noting is that the self-interest
of the decision makers themselves, as employees, is being tweaked by
Congress!

Given the excellent financial picture of both the corporations
and the pension trusts and the Congressional assault on defined
pension and "funded welfare" plans, it might be assumed that corporations are responding to new incentives.

Rival Explanations for Corporate
Change in Income Security Plans

It seems clear that the means by which these corporations have
protected the income security of retirees are changing. These corporations have responded to Congress by offering employees the opportunity
to save tax-free dollars for the future through the 401(k) and the
PAYSOP plans. Opportunities for employees to participate in profit
sharing are increasing. Also, employees have the opportunity of
purchasing their own health benefits with tax-free dollars through
cafeteria plans.

This study was based on the assumption that the Congressional
tax incentives for corporate collaboration in the retirement security
of employees has motivated decision makers to develop income protection
plans for retirees. However, rival explanations for corporate actions
exist. Incentives identified by this investigator were:
(a) Congressional tax incentives, (b) corporate human relations
philosophy, (c) union terms of agreement, (d) corporate social

responsibility ethos, (e) urgency of corporate employee recruitment, and (f) corporate competitive position.

In an effort to isolate the explanation for corporate action, the discussion of these explanations was followed by a request that the decision makers rank the rival explanations in order of importance to the corporation. The results of this question are shown in Table 4 The response of individual decision makers can be seen in Table 5.

TABLE 4

IMPORTANCE OF EXPLANATIONS
FOR CORPORATE ACTIONS

Explanation	Corporate Rank Order					
	1	2	3	4	5	6
Tax incentives	1	1	2	2	1	1
Human relations	2	4		1		1
Union terms			1	3	2	1
Social responsibility	2	1	2	1	2	
Employee recruitment	1	1	2		3	2
Competitive position	3	2	1			1

TABLE 5

RIVAL EXPLANATIONS

Corporation	Rank Order					
	1	2	3	4	5	6
Cray Research	Employee recruitment	Human relations	Tax incentives	Union terms	Social Responsibility	Competitive position
Dayton Hudson	Tax incentives	Social Responsibility	Employee recruitment			
General Mills	Social Responsibility	Tax incentives	Competitive position	Human relations	Union terms	Employee recruitment
Honeywell	Competitive position	Human relations	Union terms	Tax incentives	Employee recruitment	Social Responsibility
3M	Human relations	Competitive position	Social Responsibility	Union terms	Tax incentives	Employee recruitment
Pillsbury	Competitive position	Human relations	Tax incentives	Social Responsibility	Employee recruitment	Union terms
Super Valu	Competitive position	Human relations	Social Responsibility	Tax incentives	Employee recruitment	
Toro	Human relations	Competitive position	Employee recruitment	Union terms	Social Responsibility	Tax incentives
Wilcox Paper	Social Responsibility	Employee recruitment				

No clear pattern evolved in response to this question. Three of the informants identified "the corporate competitive position" as the most important factor in their decisions regarding the corporate plans. This was explained to the investigator as the corporation's ability to attract and retain employees, with an emphasis on "key employees."

What is interesting about this explanation is that it was not identified as one of the rival explanations in the original research proposal. Rather, this explanation became apparent to the investigator during the initial round of open-ended interviews with these decision makers. Although only three respondents ranked the corporation's competitive position as the most important explanation, this concept permeated the investigation.

Super Valu

Tax incentives are the last on the list. We don't even . . . it's not a factor for us . . . the favorable tax treatment . . . we're not in it for tax reasons. If we did not offer . . . we'd be at a distinct competitive disadvantage. Benefit plans reflect recruitment and retention . . . consistent with our philosophy.

It is interesting that this informant/respondent was not conscious of the implications of his statement. The benefits to which he alluded, that are used for retention and recruitment, ARE in fact tax subsidies. The most attractive part of the benefits for key employees and the benefit that this corporation does, in fact offer, is the avoidance of personal income tax on employer-sponsored benefits. In other words, the "wages" which this corporation offers the key

employee are subsidized by Congress. TEFRA has greatly curtailed the
privately sponsored and publicly funded benefits. The 1985 annual
reports of these corporations are evidence of their investment in such
recruitment incentives.

Toro

The informant said, "We do not attract or retain people
through compensation programs. Economics is not the prime motivator
at Toro . . . active participation [in the corporation] is the prime
motivator of the knowledge worker."

The policies at Toro certainly support the informant/
respondent's response. However, the ESOP around which the corporate
design for income security at Toro revolves enjoys a greater public
subsidy than most employee benefits for income security. ERTA and
DEFRA added to the ESOP's financial attractiveness and its attractiveness to employees. While Toro's plan predate this legislation, the
annual report for 1985 is explicit about the corporate commitment to
growth without huge capital investments. The ESOP, by increasing the
corporate working capital, is congruent with this corporate philosophy.
One can assume that the ESOP, with very special incentives for
employers and its fit with the corporate philosophy, might not be
central to the Toro design for income security in retirement without
this public subsidy.

Pillsbury

Rux had yet another perspective and ranked human relations first. "From the corporate point of view, the public image of Pillsbury which is generated by its retirees is important. Would like retirees to be proud of their past and have respect for the corporation."

The response of Rux at Pillsbury must be considered in light of his support for the generally maligned REA. This investigator suggests that although human relations may frame this respondent's point of view, the opportunity for Pillsbury to act on perceived discrimination against the young and the female employee is made possible by acts of Congress. Pillsbury, at this time, is actively adapting to the changes in the demographics and values of the work-force. The corporation and the employee are enjoying public subsidies to further this effort which is focused on the 401(k).

Honeywell

The respondent from Honeywell did see the tax incentives "as a 'subsidy', but as an end result, rather than an incentive. . . . Must find a source to fund the eighty million dollar obligation in retirement costs at Honeywell."

General Mills

The respondent from General Mills would seem to agree when he shared that "the costs for the plan are figured after the plan is established."

This seems to infer that the public subsidy for income
security plans, although it may not be the "driving force," cannot be
separated from the corporate decision to act. If the Congressional
incentive is not congruent with the corporate mission and needs, then
it is quite likely that, in these profitable and trend-setting corporations, the public subsidy would not be acted upon.

Dayton Hudson

Only the informant/respondent from Dayton Hudson named tax
incentives as the most important motivator. His position was quite
adamant. He saw tax incentives as number one, social responsibility
as number two and recruitment as 2.5. The rest he declined to rank!
He conceded that recruitment was a factor but, in his experience, he
had found that the employer was seldom called on to elaborate on the
corporate plan for a prospective employee. On the subject of tax
incentives, however, he firmly believed that:

> Without tax incentives we would address social and recruitment
> issues differently. The tax is what makes it efficient [cost
> efficient] to do something . . . if we didn't have a tax break for
> it why would we go to the hassle? . . . if we didn't have that
> efficiency, why don't we just turn around and give them additional
> compensation . . . that's deductible . . . they buy their own,
> set up their own retirement. All strictly on their own. So . . .
> tax is number one . . . without that piece it's not efficient.

A close look at exactly what this informant/respondent is
saying seems to be the Congressional purpose restated! Consider "if
we didn't have a tax break for it why should we go to the hassle?"
Congressional action, through TEFRA, has limited the tax incentives
for the integration of the corporate plan and Social Security. It has

also limited the personal tax subsidy for the key employee. This has undermined the utility of pensions as corporate incentives.

In addition, the public subsidy for pensions has been undermined by REA which increased pension plan participation by lowering the age for inclusion from twenty-five to twenty-one. This means higher PBGC cost. The cost of corporate benefits has also been increased by the new, shorter and female-specific vesting schedules mandated by REA. Higher corporate costs have translated into lower public subsidies. That is, there are some benefits for which the corporation IS no longer getting a tax break.

In light of Hamacher's remarks, it hardly seems coincidental that all the large corporations now report a decrease in their interest in pension plans. Prior to TEFRA, qualified defined pensions plans were the favored and established response to the retirement income question in all the large corporations.

Next, consider the statement, " . . . give them additional compensation . . . they can buy their own retirement." The opportunity to do this seems to be exactly what Congress did with the passage of the Revenue Act. This Act gave the corporations the 401(k). Corporations now have the opportunity to offer employees an "efficient" means for increasing wages through employer contribution. In addition, employees now have the opportunity to "buy their own retirement security" by saving tax-free dollars. DEFRA also gave the employee a tax subsidy for wisely selecting health benefits through cafeteria plans. At the same time, Congress limited the public subsidy for employer-sponsored deferred compensation in the form of insurance and health care benefits.

It is no secret that the 401(k) savings plans and the cafeteria plans which offer health benefits are new and popular additions to the corporate plans for the economic and social security of retirees. It is also no secret that these decision makers have found the structural changes made by DEFRA in the corporate method for funding welfare benefits restrictive. These restrictions and the associated corporate costs, together with the decrease in the public subsidy, are subjects of active debate where decisions on retirement income are being made.

The informant from Dayton Hudson seemed to put "the handwriting on the wall." Tax incentives or disincentives are, indeed, an important variable in the decisions made regarding the plans for retirement income security.

Discussion

The explanation of what motivates the corporations to develop retirement income plans probably cannot be ascribed to a single variable. Rather, there appears to be a "family" of motivators to which these decision makers respond. In each case, decisions will be individualized by the nature of the corporation. The changing demographics of the workforce are particularly important at this time to General Mills and Pillsbury, both of whom have new and substantial commitments to the restaurant and fast foods business. As these informants have pointed out, for the corporation to "get a bang for the buck," plans must reflect the needs and values of the employees.

The philosophy of the corporation is also an important variable. This is evident in the corporations such as Toro and Cray Research where the value of employee self-determination and participation for the "knowledge worker" shape the corporate philosophies and, so, the policies. At corporations such as 3M and Honeywell, the "corporate family" concept is predominant and decisions reflect a more paternalistic philosophy. On the other hand, the evidence suggests that, together with the corporate demographics and philosophy, preferential tax treatment as a way to subsidize corporate costs has played a major role in decisions to offer employees access to a retirement income security plans.

It is questionable that these corporations would tolerate the ERISA standards, the authority of the IRS over plan design and execution, and the seemingly arbitrary Congress, if the tax incentives were not an important decision making variable.

Income Security Updates in
Three Large Corporations

When this study was initiated, the corporate decision makers suggested that the timing of the study was two years too soon. In 1986 the corporate compensation managers had many questions about deferred compensations but had made few decisions. The investigator was particularly curious about what direction Pillsbury might take.

Pillsbury

At the time of the interviews at Pillsbury, the investigator
noted that the pension trust fund assumption had been changed from
8.5 percent in 1985 to ten percent in 1986. The trust fund assumption
refers to the rate of pension trust fund growth, anticipated by the
corporation. If the assumption is low, say 7.5 percent as at Dayton
Hudson, the corporation might contribute a higher amount to cover
pension liabilities that are due. If the rate is high, such as
Pillsbury's, then the corporate contributions to meet pension
liabilities are relatively low.

When trust fund assumptions are relatively high, or change
unexpectedly, this is considered an indicator that the corporation may
either be planning to terminate the pension plan or that the corporation is in financial straights and cannot afford to meet the
liabilities coming due.

It seemed apparent from the annual report that the Pillsbury
profit picture was healthy. This left the investigator curious about
the reason for the change. There were several small differences at
Pillsbury. The informant at Pillsbury also was the only one to speak
positively about the proposed five-year vesting of pension benefits
that was being proposed by the Tax Reform Act. He also had an
unexpected enthusiasm for the 401(k), even suggesting that Social
Security be built on the same principles! Also unusual, the age of
participation in the 401(k) was established at eighteen. This was
somewhat surprising because of the rate of turnover one would expect

in the fast food industry. Most corporations with a high percentage
of young first-hires are cautious about including these employees
immediately in the 401(k). The reason for this is that the corporate
discrimination ratio required by the IRS may be jeopardized. It
should be noted here that these ratios are "negotiated" by each
corporation with the IRS. One can assume that if the IRS "street
level bureaucrat" approved of the intent of a corporate income
security plan that then a more flexible discrimination ratio would be
approved. Coupled with this low age for participation was a corporate
contribution based on the employee's salary.

These assorted bits of information deviated somewhat from the
norm. This suggested to the investigator that the corporate goal of
employee retention, associated with the current defined pension plan,
might no longer have utility for the corporation.

A final interview with the compensation manager at Pillsbury in
the fall of 1987 found the corporation looking at new approaches to
income security in retirement--approaches that would meet the needs of
a new population of employees. The pension plan at Pillsbury was
twenty-six years old. When the plans were introduced the employees
were older and less mobile. Also, Pillsbury was not in the restaurant
business. Employees are now younger and more mobile. A major consideration of this decision maker was that in two years only two employees
from the restaurant group became eligible for pension benefits. Also,
the corporation had long realized that it was generating very little
public relations among employees with its pension plan. The

corporate goals now are to maximize portability and so address the needs of a younger workforce. It is also interested in developing a plan that will give the corporation a "bang for the buck."

At the time of the interview, the informant was sure that Pillsbury would "tweak" the corporate design to favor defined contributions over a defined benefits plan. No decisions had been made at the time of the interview. It was interesting that one of the alternatives mentioned was a carbon copy of the plan at Toro, that is, a defined contribution plan based on Employee Stock Option Plans and combined with a pension benefit floor. This implies the opportunity of stock ownership for employees as well as the portability of benefits for employees who wish to change employers. It also guarantees some level of retirement security for those employees who make a career of service to Pillsbury.

This discussion of retirement benefits also included a discussion of the search at Pillsbury for a new measure of reward--one that was not tied to the traditional "ladder of success" but a system which could reward employees for lateral moves. The informant made it clear that they were discussing a measure other than regular increases in wages and/or a hierarchy of positions within the company. The investigator was left wondering if this were in part a result of TEFRA and the implied measure of adequacy expressed in that legislation.

Dayton Hudson

The interview with Pillsbury piqued the investigator's curiosity about how other corporations were responding to the Tax

Reform Act. This led to a telephone contact with Hamacher at Dayton
Hudson. The investigator made this choice because this informant/
respondent was philosophically committed to the defined benefit
plan. He was, however, very frustrated with the newly legislated
restrictions, with the PBGC costs and the constant changes in IRS
rules and standards. Also, his statement that five-year vesting was
only "termination pay" suggested to the investigator that TRACT's
shortened vesting schedule might have had a major impact on the plans
at Dayton Hudson.

Dayton Hudson, too, is in a state of indecision. Hamacher
said it has considered "getting out of defined benefit completely."
This would and could be accomplished by terminating the defined
benefit plan and vesting all the participants (not required by law,
but certainly ethical, and good for the public image!). This would be
done by buying annuities for the amount of the accrued benefits. The
timing of such a move would be appropriate because the pension trust
which is overfunded could bear the cost. Also, corporations with over-
funded pension trusts that have adopted the FASB 1987 rule have
generated income by allowing corporations to amortize the difference
between pension trust assets and the promised liabilities of the plan.

Hamacher did agonize over the fact that philosopically, in his
opinion, a change to defined contribution was "not right." His
concern was based on the risk factor involved for the employee in
developing retirement security. He was not convinced that some
paternalism is not necessary. That is, he gave recognition to the

doctrine of "moral obligation" of the employer to prevent "financial injury" (Chambers, 1980). About the ability of the average individual to plan for retirement, Hamacher commented that, "I wish I could say that people are changing but they're not."

In response to the question about whether or not Dayton Hudson had considered the floor plan, he said that it had. The problem of the floor plan for this decision maker was the $8.50 PBGC cost for each participant which makes the plan less than efficient, and the attendant ERISA rules and regulations that corporations would be required to meet. The uncertainty about how high the PBGC costs will go will be an important factor in any decision at Dayton Hudson.

One plan being considered by Hamacher is the "target benefit plan." This plan avoids PBGC costs because it is perceived as a defined contribution plan. A target benefit, which is the same as a benefit in a defined benefit plan, is payable at normal retirement age. This plan can be a final average salary benefit and can take past service into account. The target plans can also be integrated with Social Security--a cost efficient feature which would be bound to attract this informant! A target income, much the same as a floor, guarantees retirement income. This mitigates the risks for the employee that are inherent in the defined contribution plans. Such a plan would also avoid much of the regulation of defined benefit plans. This plan is portable because of the "personal account" or defined contribution feature. This plan would better suit the needs of the

Dayton Hudson employee population, where longevity with the corporation only averages 2.5 years, than the current plan, based on a
thirty-year career.

Given the nature of the employee population at Dayton Hudson
the investigator has the sense that, like Pillsbury, the old plan is
no longer serving the needs of both the young mobile employees and the
mature corporation. Some compromise plan will need to be developed.
From past experience with the 401(k) it can also be assumed that when
the decision is made, action will be swift!

With the knowledge that the decision maker at Dayton Hudson
considers the tax incentives the number one motivator for corporate
plan design, it can be anticipated that new plans will reflect the
Congressional purpose!

General Mills

According to General Mills' 1985 annual report, the corporation underwent "an historic restructuring" to emphasize consumer foods
and restaurants. This implies a change, also, in the demographics of
the employee population. This knowledge, plus the fact that this
informant was actively involved in discussions with the members of
Congress on matters of retirement income indicated that a follow-up
interview might prove instructive. The investigator was not
disappointed.

General Mills was actively involved in changing the structure
of the corporate plan. Some of the pension benefits were being

terminated and replaced with defined contribution plans. According to
this informant, Congress had "exceeded" the "balance point." Richie
thought it possible that General Mills might eventually "get out of
the pension business completely."

Discussion

These three corporations can be considered leaders in the
business community, locally and nationally. It seems safe to assume
that these corporations might set new trends and new standards for
employee retirement benefits. If that happens, those corporations
that want to stay "competitive" can be expected to follow suit.

The decision makers still did not articulate a perception that
the Congressional "dog was wagging the corporate tail." These informants conveyed the impression that the "corporate dog was wagging the
Congressional tail." The informants, with the exception of Pillsbury,
indicated that the demands of Congress, with DEFRA and REA and now
TRACT, had exceeded the limits that would be tolerated by the corporation. In response, these decision makers were terminating or limiting
the historic collaboration with Congress in achieving a goal of income
security for retirees through pension benefits. In either case, the
Congressional purpose, as interpreted by this investigator, was being
realized.

CHAPTER VI

DISCUSSION

This study was undertaken to answer the question of the impact
of tax incentives on corporate income security plans for retirees by
examining the reactions of nine corporations (six large and three
small) to the following Acts of Congress: (a) the Revenue Act, 1978,
(b) the Economic Recovery Tax Act (ERTA), 1981, (c) the Tax Equity and
Fiscal Responsibility Act (TEFRA), 1982, (d) the Deficit Reduction Act
(DEFRA), 1984 and (e) the Retirement Equity Act (REA), 1984. The
Titmuss model, which broadly defines welfare to include fiscal,
occupational and social benefits, was used to analyze the study
findings.

Corporate Change

Large Corporations

The influence of tax incentives is most evident when the
behavior of the six large corporations of this study is compared with
that of the three small corporations. Before the passage of TEFRA,
the first act in the history of Congress to discourage the development
of private pension plans, all the large corporations sponsored these
plans as the primary vehicle for the income protection of their
retirees.

Following TEFRA, DEFRA and REA, the large corporations reported a change in the corporate focus from pension plans to defined contribution plans. By 1987 General Mills, Dayton Hudson and Pillsbury were actively engaged in dismantling pension plans in favor of defined contribution or profit-share plans. This move to defined contribution plans represents structural changes in the design of these corporate plans as well as changes in the funding patterns. An incongruence of purpose, and a subsequent search for congruence, is implied between Congress and the large corporations through their response to tax disincentives.

Small Corporations

All the small corporations sponsored defined contribution plans as the source of income protection for their retirees. Therefore, the Congressional acts did not cause the three small corporations to make any structural changes or to change their methods of funding plans. This absence of structural change in the corporations that sponsored defined contribution plans implies a congruence between the purpose of Congress and the corporations. For that reason, the disincentives applied by Congress for plans that focused on income security plans did not apply.

Key Variables

Three variables--(a) the corporate philosophy and mission, (b) the demographics of corporate employees and (c) the source of funding--associated with the tax incentives were found to play

interdependent roles in corporate decision making regarding income
security plans.

Corporate Philosophy and Mission

Each of the study's informants expressed sensitivity to the
image portrayed by the corporation to the community through its
retirees. Pride was frequently expressed in the trust of the
employees for the corporation. In addition, the corporate plans have
the dual purpose of protecting the income of retirees and keeping the
corporations' competitive in attracting key personnel. The mission of
these corporations defines how this perquisite will be used. This is
evident at General Mills and Pillsbury where restructuring of the corporation has meant a change in the nature of personnel who are
rewarded. Consequently, the corporate plans are changing. At Super
Valu the acquisition of Shopko has led them to offer a dual approach
to income protection to better meet the needs of the younger Shopko
employees and the older, more traditional warehouse personnel. On the
other hand, at 3M and Honeywell, who are more paternalistic and still
interested in employee retention, the change in focus has been less
dramatic.

Demographics of Corporate Employees

Changes in the demographics of the employee groups studied
here reflect the national trend to younger more mobile employees. The
change is most apparent in the corporations that focus on retail sales
and restaurants. These young employees as a group are new to these

corporations, except Dayton Hudson. They express little interest in corporate pension plans contingent on thirty-year careers.

Pensions have little value as a perquisite to attract key employees nor, according to these decision makers, do pension generally have currency as a corporate benefit. Dayton Hudson, General Mills and Pillsbury are all seeking new plans which will better reflect the needs of this younger more mobile group. The small corporations have only moved to make their plans richer, either with the 401(k) or increased profit-sharing.

Source of Funding

Congressional tax incentives serve to subsidize the funding of the income security plans in these corporations and are seen as important to the general revenue picture. At this time, it appears that the revenue picture for the large corporations has benefited from the synergy generated by a combination of over-funded pension trusts and the adoption of the FASB 1987 rule, which has allowed these corporations to amortize the difference between pension trust assets and the promised liabilities of the plan. This will facilitate a corporation's change from a plan which agrees to finance a future promise in retirement to a plan that annually meets employee obligations. With funding available to make the switch from a promise-to-pay supported by an established pension trust to pay-as-you-go plan based on annual profits in these major corporations, change has become a financial possibility. Concommitantly, the Congressional disincentives coupled

with new incentives to change are more attractive given this corporate
revenue picture.

These three variables have created a climate in these large
corporations which is conducive to change from pensions as the primary
source of income protection for retirees. This climate is most
apparent at Dayton Hudson, General Mills and Pillsbury but is also
present to a lesser degree at Honeywell, 3M and Super Valu.

Changes in Retirement Income Security

Employees

The change in the relationship between pension plans and
defined contribution plans that is taking place in these corporations
has significant implications for the employee and the corporation.
The employee's accrued assets in defined contribution plans, in
contrast to pension plans, are, by statute, immediately vested.
Employees can capture the corporation contributions immediately at Cray
Research and within a range of two to five years at the other corporations. This means that at corporations where defined contribution
plans are the primary vehicle for income security in retirement, the
employee cannot be held hostage by the promise of future benefits.
These employees will not suffer economically if they terminate service
with the corporation, since accrued assets are portable between
employers. The corporation, as a consequence, has no future pension
promise by which to attract key employees or encourage retention. New
ways to meet the competitive challenge are currently being explored by

these decision makers. The implications are that those new ways will focus on the present conditions of employment, rather than future retirement, as do pension plans.

While corporate choices will be limited by putting accrued assets in the control of employees through personal accounts, the employee's opportunities and choices will have been increased. The price paid for this increased opportunity is an increased responsibility for individual income protection in the future. The corporate decision makers in the large corporations are not convinced that the average employee is concerned enough about the future to fully exploit the opportunities offered by profit-share plans. On the other hand, in the small corporations the informants expressed confidence in the employees' ability to make independent decisions.

The Toro experience suggests that lower-level employees need some protection against the vagaries of the bond and investment market. The current discussions at Dayton Hudson, General Mills and Pillsbury are focussing on plans which include a pension as a minimum defined benefit similar to the model designed by Toro. This is consistent with the importance placed on the corporate community image by these decision makers. A combination of these plans will increase the financial independence of the employee from the corporation in the present, as well as guarantee the employee an adequate pension in retirement if the employee should stay.

Savings

The wholesale adoption of the 401(k) savings plans by all but
one of these corporations and the reported growing interest of
employee participation has further increased the financial independence of the employee. Unlike the Individual Retirement Account (IRA),
the accrued assets of a 401(k) can be retrieved under special circumstances which makes savings attractive to young employees who cannot
predict the future. This popular savings plan can be seen as a
statutory contract between the employee and Congress. This contract
has changed the nature of savings from a reduction of wages to an
increase in wages through tax incentives now directly available to the
employee. Congress now is directly subsidizing the salaries of
unorganized employees who save wages for their retirement. This sets
the 401(k) apart from other occupational welfare benefits.

Employers have found a new tax-sheltered perquisite in the
401(k) which also reduces corporate payroll taxes. In those corporations where the mission and/or the technology is changing and early
retirement is in the best interest of the corporation, the 401(k), in
the absence of the traditional tax shelters for income, has become a
corporate incentive for early retirement. Congress is thus subsidizing the early retirement policies of the corporations in this study.

Plan Design

The 401(k) is an attractive economic benefit for employees.
For employers the 401(k) is attractive from an economic standpoint, as
a tax-sheltered perquisite and as a mechanism for profit-sharing.

The coupling of this opportunity for employees to save tax-free dollars with the vesting and portability benefits of a defined contribution plan is redefining deferred compensation in the corporations.

Traditionally, deferred compensation and retirement benefits were seen as synonymous. In recent years early retirement policies in these corporations, built on generous tax subsidies, have changed the patterns of employment on which the concepts of deferred compensation and retirement were originally established. Now, according to the respondent from General Mills where the average retirement age is fifty years of age, "No one retires at sixty-five anymore." Similar patterns were found in other corporations. On the other hand, the promised retirement benefits are not sacrificed, but are rearranged. What was retirement FROM work at sixty-five now has the potential of being "retirement TO something different." The employee who chooses early retirement for whatever reason does so with the knowledge that retirement benefits are protected in the present and in the future.

This encroachment on the concept of income protection in post-work retirement is also reflected in the trend encouraged by Congress toward defined contribution plans rather than pension benefits,and the defining characteristics of the 401(k). Now "retirement" is becoming synonymous with "termination pay." According to the informant from Dayton Hudson, pension vesting schedules proposed by Congress upset the actuarial formulae and more closely reflect termination pay than pension benefits.

The combination of a defined contribution plan and a 401(k)
savings plan gives the employee the opportunity to protect post-work
income. In addition, immediate vesting of the employee's accrued
benefits, short vesting schedules for employer contributions, portability between employers and savings plan subsidized by Congress add
to the income security of participating employees in the present.
This pre-retirement income security of employees changes the relationship of the employee to the employer. In a sense, the legislation has made retirement voluntary. The voluntary nature of retirement is epitomized in the contemporary design for income security at
Cray Research. There is no vesting of employer contributions and the
philosophical focus of the corporate benefits plan is on "Life After
Cray" rather than retention.

The Titmuss Model

Titmuss identified fiscal and occupational benefits as
welfare, a function of the nation's dual tax system. He contended
that welfare must be defined by the purpose served and the benefit
distributed rather than by the means of delivery. This redefinition
seems to give a more accurate picture of economic and social distribution in the modern welfare state. Private income security plans
qualify as occupational welfare, according to Titmuss, because the
objective, to protect the income of retirees, matches that of the
welfare state.

Occupational Welfare

The premise that occupational benefits are welfare is not universally accepted. However, the nine corporations studied here meet the Titmuss criteria. With the exception of Wilcox Paper, all these corporations have formally organized compensation and benefits departments responsible for designing plans that will protect the income of employees during post-work years. In addition, all but Wilcox Paper employ their own legal counsel to translate and operationalize the standards, rules and changes legislated by Congress that affect the delivery of this benefit to the participants. The importance of income security benefits to the corporate competitive position expressed by these informants suggests that other corporations probably follow suit.

In addition, Congress is explicit about the role of private employers as collaborators in attaining the economic well-being of the nation's elderly. This partnership is further reflected by the fact that all these corporations offer their employees "defined and qualified" benefits. This entitles the corporation, by statute, to an economic subsidy based on the corporate tax obligation and entitles the employee to the protection of the standards and rules of the state. This collaboration is also manifested in seven of these corporations through the integration of pension plans with Social Security benefits. Clearly, the manifest purpose of income security plans in these corporations is congruent with the purpose of the state to protect the economic income of the nation's aged.

Prior to this study, Root (1982) found occupational welfare
in the Inland Steel Corporation to be a governmentally encouraged,
public-private hybrid for the delivery of benefits. Like Titmuss,
Root also found that the "most enduring impact has come from federal
tax law" (p. 48). This study would support Root's observations.
First, the income security plans looked at here represent a public-
private hybrid. This concept has been significantly reinforced with
the recent legislation. Second, the tax laws have an enduring impact.
Congress first supported private pension development in 1921. Not
until 1982 were there any legislative changes affecting the tax-
favored status of this benefit. Concommitantly, the older established corporations reported that their pension policies had remained
essentially unchanged. Ambromovitz (1981), using the Titmuss framework, found that "almost everyone is on welfare" when the tax expense
system is analyzed. It is difficult to see how these benefits, given
the work of these scholars and the results of this study, can be
defined other than as occupational welfare for the benefit of the
employees' income security.

Dual Tax System

When Titmuss first identified occupational welfare in 1958 and
taxes as social purpose acts, he used the analogy of the iceberg. The
submerged portion was representative of fiscal and occupational benefits channelled through tax expenditures. He found that distribution
of the welfare state's resources in this manner was an "alternative to

legislated social policy" and that these resources go beyond the support of dependency to opportunities for individual self-improvement.

Congress has since (1967) recognized tax expenditures as a budget item. The subsequent passage of the 1974 Congressional Budget Act in 1974 has officially recognized both tax expenditures and tax appropriations as legitimate forms of distribution in the welfare state. If occupational social work is indeed welfare, then it can no longer be seen as social action that is an alternative to the legislated social policy. Occupational welfare is, in fact, legislated social policy that takes place outside the legislative purview of tax appropriations. This, in fact, puts the large corporations with large sums of tax expenses at their disposal in the position of being quasi-public, as is the voluntary sector of social welfare. The tax incentive, or subsidy, available to each of these corporations for distribution through income security plans is analogous to the grants now available to voluntary human service agencies.

Not only are tax expenditures recognized, they have grown in importance from 4.4 percent of the Gross National Product (GNP) in 1967 to 8.4 percent of the GNP in 1982. It has been found more recently that out of one hundred dollars that Congress appropriated, Congress "expensed" sixty-five dollars (Social Security Bulletin, April 1987, p. 7). This study as well as the work of Root and Ambromovitz have noted the distribution of welfare benefits through this increasingly important system.

These findings are particularly interesting in light of the discussions by Rein (1977) and Miller (1985) of the "doctrine of overload" besetting the modern welfare states. This is the question of how modern welfare states can be politically redefined to meet increasing social and economic obligations. Most welfare states have found that further expansion of the tax appropriations pie for social distribution is no longer possible. The findings of this investigation suggest that the tax expense system is the Congressional RESPONSE to the dilemma presented in the doctrine of overload. That is, the tax expense system has become an increasingly important and politically viable means for economic and social distribution in the welfare state. The findings of this study identify the corporate income security plans and the 401(k) savings plan as models of the Congressional use of the tax expense system to promote Miller's socially motivated economic policies. A criterion for institutionalized welfare is that the delivery be subject to public oversight. The detailed IRS form 5500 required of all but one of these corporations goes both to the Department of Labor and to the Treasury Department and is a documented record of the corporate compliance over the past year, which can be challenged at any time by the IRS, and is available to the public.

To support this investigator's perception of the tax expense system as an alternate and important source of economic and social distribution, a review of the changes taking place in these corporations is instructive. As a result of the Congressional tax incentives, the Revenue Act is encouraging and enticing the development of tax-free savings plans for employees through the tax expense incentives in all but one of these corporations. The Economic Recovery Tax Act encourages and entices the development of individual savings through tax credits plus employee ownership of their means of employment through the payroll tax system. Toro is taking advantage of the special tax incentives offered through ESOPs and Pillsbury is thinking of doing the same. The tax expense system, in this case, has encouraged these employers to participate with Congress in democratizing the workplace. Congress further encourages employee participation in their economic welfare with TEFRA and DEFRA. Congress withdrew economic incentives from paternalistic employers who promised economic security in the future through pensions to exchange for incentives designed to give employees the opportunity to be self-determining in questions of economic security in the present. All the corporations are responding, although at different rates. Finally, with the passage of REA, Congress made economic incentives contingent upon social values that impact the well-being of the nation's families. All these corporations must now recognize marriage as an economic partnership, the unique patterns of employment of women and the concept of androgyny in the workplace.

This identificiation of the importance of the tax expense system in the delivery of welfare can be applied to observations made by Miller (1985). He found that the contemporary welfare state will be powered by Post-Keynesian economics. This theory rejects the study of how to allocate the welfare state's scarce resources. Rather, Post-Keynesian economics is the study of how an economic system can be expanded to produce and distribute a social surplus. The metaphor of the welfare state's resource pie is exchanged by this investigator for a metaphor of a loaf of bread. Instead of Congress cutting the pie in as many pieces as possible, yeast is added to the bread dough in proportion to the size loaf required to meet economic and social needs. See Appendix B for a more detailed explanation of this metaphor.

This study suggests that the complex relationship of Congress to these corporations represents a model of Post-Keynesian economics. It is evident that the economic system has been expanded by tax incentives to produce and distribute a social surplus. This "surplus" is represented by the corporate and employee resources capatured for the deferred compensation plans. The capture of these social purpose dollars was affected by the tax incentive legislated by Congress.

If the hallmark of Post-Keynesian economics is the study of how an economic system can expand to produce and distribute a social surplus then the tax expense system appears to represent a model of the new economic theory identified by Miller. Of particular interest to social policy analysis is Miller's finding that this theory will serve to describe and explain the evolving welfare state. If Miller is correct, this fresh awareness and new perspective on the dual tax system may generate economic and social policies in the future which serve the evolution of the welfare state.

Equity

Scholars have found equal and equitable distribution difficult to achieve in occupational welfare. Root (1982) found that the distribution of welfare through the employer increased inequities between citizens by creating an "enclave" of privileged beneficiaries. Nelson (1983) found that fiscal, occupational and social welfare together have served to distribute an inequitable share of the state's resources to the elderly. Titmuss was critical of occupational welfare because he found it contingent on the employee's status, merit and need which he found to further exacerbate inequity in the welfare state.

This study confirms Root's findings that occupational welfare results in enclaves of privileged beneficiaries. The income security plans studied here applied only to "salaried" employees. The IRS discrimination rules are applied selectively by groups which means that participation must be fair only within the group. The popular 401(k), although it represents a contract between Congress and the employee, is by statute unavailable to organized labor. This will serve to further discriminate between employees. In addition, the use of the 401(k) as an incentive for key level employees and as an incentive for retirement will increase the inequities between retirees. Further, this benefit is only available through the discretion of the employer. Although only one corporation in this group failed to offer this benefit to employees, only 6 percent of all the nation's workers are covered under employer-sponsored 401(k)s. (Copies of Pensions:

Worker Coverage and Retirement Income, 1984, Series P-70, No. 12, will
be available from the Superintendent of Documents, U.S. Government
Printing Office, Washington, D.C. 20402.) In the case of the 401(k)
the discrimination must be laid at the feet of Congress which developed
this benefit and then chose to bow to union pressure and limited
employee access.

The Congressional encouragement of corporations to replace
pension plans with defined contribution plans may well be placing
responsibility for income security in the future on those employees
least likely to be able to plan for the future. Traditionally, it is
the smaller, newer, less secure corporation that will offer defined
contribution plans. This was also true in this study although the
corporations were financially secure. The less secure corporations
are unlikely to consider sharing the risks as does Toro, nor are the
wages likely to be as generous as the small corporations studied here.

Scholars since Titmuss have focused on identifying the problems of inequity created by distribution through occupational welfare.
In the process, some of the opportunities of increasing creative
justice, defined by Titmuss as the individual's right of access to
resources of the welfare state, have been overlooked. Root found
occupational welfare generous and non-stigmatizing; Ambromovitz found
fiscal welfare generous, stigma-free and humane; Nelson found that the
elderly were being served inequitably well through a combination of
fiscal, occupational and social welfare. In this study, it was found
that occupational welfare benefits contingent on the employer

relationship with Congress could create employee opportunity through
financial security in the pre-retirement years and could free the
employee from a relationship to an employer contingent on long-term
employment. Congress, having made benefits contingent on corporate
behavior, can also be deliberately egalitarian, as demonstrated by REA.

Few scholars have fully explored or exploited the advantages
of occupational welfare. Rather, scholars have focused on identifying the encroachment of fiscal and occupational welfare on what has
been considered the potential resources of a conceptually and struc-
turally "compartmentalized" social welfare system.

Change

This study of the relationship of corporations to the
Congressional tax acts identifies the amazing tolerance for change in
large, trend-setting and technologically sophisticated corporations.
All the corporations, except for Wilcox Paper, operationalized the
myriad of changes imposed by Congress from 1982 to 1985. This does
not take into consideration major bills not discussed here which
impacted the corporate funded welfare plans.

Titmuss has identified change as the only constant in the
modern welfare state. These corporations demonstrated an ability to
absorb the changes mandated and encouraged by Congress. New plans
were rapidly put in place, as was demonstrated by the Dayton Hudson
development of the 401(k) plan. In addition, if Congressional intent,
such as the encouragement of defined contribution plans, is in the
interest of the corporation at large, as it was Pillsbury's, the

organization does not tolerate or maintain institutional loyalties to entrenched policies as often seen in human service agencies. An example drawn from personal experience would be the effort to refocus the care of the developmentally disabled from institutional care to community care. In some cases, human service policy change takes a generation of employees!

Congress has demonstrated the ability to reshape the corporate response to income security needs of retirees. This calls for the vigilant eye of the concerned policy proponent of the welfare state. Congress is not always just, as in the case of the 401(k), and whether or not Congress is right is always a matter of debate. However, in a rapidly changing and complexly organized society, this ability to rapidly reflect the purpose of the welfare state through the tax expense system and occupational welfare has considerable potential for exploitation by social policy proponents.

Implications for Further Study

When this study was initiated the executive at General Mills was interested but thought the study was two years ahead of its time. It was his opinion that by 1988 dramatic changes would be taking place in corporate compensation and benefits planning. This study only addresses the alternatives that these decision makers were considering, and the reasoning upon which their responses were based, as they considered new legislation. With this in mind, the following topics are discussed: (1) a follow-up study, (2) retirement as voluntary, (3) income security over the life-span, (4) equity in employee deferred compensation, (5) health benefits, (6) theories of the welfare state and (7) the corporation as a quasi-public institution.

1. It would seem useful to conduct a follow-up study, covering the years 1985 to 1990, to challenge or affirm the findings reported here, and to determine exactly how these corporations implemented the policies operationalized by the acts of Congress. Scholars could then compare the new approaches to income security for retirees with past approaches, using measures of proportional and creative equity and adequacy, as defined by Titmuss. Such a study would help to inform and to evaluate the viability of the market and the tax expense system as a means of social distribution in a modern welfare state.

2. This investigator refers to the years 1975-1985 as the "'Congress' decade of the employee." This nomenclature was based on Congress' focus on the rights of employees and the subsequent implications of this focus. This study finds that the concept of "retirement" as an institution appears to be undergoing fundamental change. In technologically sophisticated companies such as Cray Research, retirement was in fact "voluntary" and accepted corporate policy and "culture". That is, the concept of "retirement", with the help of acts of Congress, is giving way to that of "separation" based on the employee's choice, with no negative financial consequences for the employee. Also, the mature corporations studied no longer saw sixty-five as the "normal" retirement age, and were eliminating some negative financial consequences of "early retirement". It is

suggested that employees now may be retiring "to" new fields, aided in part by the 401(k), rather than "from" corporate positions, based on conditions of tenure. This phenomenon of retiring to other work has been referred to as the fourth leg of the well-balanced income security stool. Income security issues have always been of major importance to the social work profession. New information on how employees are planning for future employment and economic security would inform scholars at a time when Congress has contracted directly with the employee through the 401(k) pre-tax income savings benefit.

3. The cosmological approach of Congress, the corporate response and the demographics of the employee in the modern post-industrial welfare state, has introduced a "preventive, family-based" concept of "income security over the life-time" in preference to a single focus of "income security in retirement". An investigation of the employee response to changes in deferred compensation plans would determine if access to, and portability of, deferred wages has increased the life-time income security and had utility for the modern mobile employees and their families.

4. It is well established that retirement plans represent an employee's deferred wages. It is also well established that the corporate risk factor and the financial contribution to defined benefits plans is seen as greater than the employer risk and financial contribution to defined contribution/profit-sharing plans.

In those corporations where defined contributions will replace defined benefit plans as the major emphasis of deferred compensation assets, will the employee's compensation increase to reflect the reduced costs to the corporation and the increase in risk to the employee? Empirical evidence will be necessary to answer this question of equity in the distribution of profits.

5. Health is increasingly fragile as one grows older. Health benefits were mentioned but not discussed in this study. The economic security of retired persons depends a great deal on the health benefits available to them. Many corporations have invested heavily in this benefit for employees. However, the Deficit Reduction Act began an assault on the corporate ability to efficiently provide "funded welfare" plans. To add to the financial burden of corporations, in 1985 Congress passed the Consolidated Omnibus Budget Reconciliation Act (COBRA), designed to reduce gaps in health care benefits for employees who were laid off, retired, or otherwise separated from employments.

COBRA is consistent with the concept of the employee's "income security over the life span." Congress required employers who maintain health insurance plans to continue to terminated workers for up to eighteen months. This act of Congress has in fact extended the meaning of the term "employee" to mean someone no longer actively employed by the sponsor of a health plan. COBRA has significantly changed the relationship of the employer to the health care delivery system.

The informant from General Mills indicated that restricting the corporate ability to pre-fund health benefits was not popular. Many of the informants were angry about the extended social

obligations imposed by COBRA. Social work professionals would benefit
from knowing how corporations are responding to the health policy
mandates of Congress. Benefits enjoyed during retirement become a
status right. For this reason it is increasingly important that
employees retire with benefits that adequately supplement the public
programs. Research on how corporations implement Congressional
mandates would serve to inform the profession about the distribution
of health benefits and provide direction for social planning and
political advocacy.

6. In 1967 Congress recognized tax expenditures as a budget
item. With passage of the 1974 Congressional Budget Act tax expenditures were officially recognized as a legitimate form of redistribution
in the modern welfare state. Occupational welfare then can no longer
be viewed as an "alternative to legislated social policy." Rather,
occupational welfare must be perceived as the result of distribution
through an alternate means by Congress. To insure that the democratic
principles of the welfare state are served policy analysts will need
to recognized and understand these means.

This study suggests that the dual tax system identified by
Titmuss may be a representation of Keynsian and Post-Keynesian economic
theories. If this is so, then tax appropriations and tax expenditures
will be based on quite different assumptions and hence different means.
This investigator has suggested that the metaphor of the "resource pie"
fails to depict and explain tax expenditures. This alternate system
by which Congress distributes the resources of the welfare state is

better represented by perceiving tax incentives as the process by which yeast creates and regulates the size of a loaf of bread.

A study which examines tax expenditures based on the assumptions of Post-Keynesian economics would serve to more accurately evaluate whether or not the modern welfare state is using two distinct but legitimate means to distribute resources among citizens, and whether or not the democratic goals of the welfare state are being advanced by so doing.

7. Big corporations are in the position to have large sums of tax expense money, or social purpose dollars, at their disposal for the development of employee benefits. If the broader definition of welfare proposed by Titmuss is accepted, then the corporations become the means for the distribution of welfare. This puts the corporation in the position of being a quasi-public institution, as in the voluntary welfare sector in the United States. The tax incentives, or subsidies, available to corporations for distribution through income security plans are analogous to the public dollars now available to voluntary human service organizations for the delivery of social welfare.

If the corporation can be considered a quasi-public institution, then the well-established criteria of social welfare institutions (Wilensky and Lebeau, 1965), accepted by most social work professionals, will need to be reexamined. Further study here might expand the conceptual boundaries within which social policy analysta and proponents have worked.

Conclusion

This investigation found that the fundamentals of funding and administration of social welfare have been too narrowly conceived and perceived. The funding and administration of social services in a developing welfare state is now, and has been, a question of "either-or": either tax appropriations or tax expenditures.

This duality of means has utility and is congruent with the social work profession's concern for meeting the needs of BOTH the socially dependent and the socially independent citizens. This dual system is also consistent with the prevailing ecological-life social work practice model's focus on client situations, client empowerment and the prevention of economic/social problems.

If the findings of this study are valid, then a new and holistic configuration of questions will need to be asked by social policy analysts and proponents for the democratic principles of the state to be preserved, advanced and expanded.

APPENDIX A

LEGISLATIVE HISTORY

Richard Titmuss was critical of the American welfare state as the only modern industrialized nation to base income security for the aged on both market criteria and need. In the United States the distribution of resources through labor force participation plays an important role in the welfare state.

Occupational welfare, in the form of income security plans for retirement, is available to employees of organizations interested in deferring compensation for their employees. The American employers have collaborated with the Congress to develop a significant source of privately sponsored, work-related, income security system for retirees. These income security plans cost the government fifty billion dollars in foregone taxes in 1985 (Reich, 1987). At the same time, private employers paid out ninety billion dollars in retirement income to fifteen million recipients (Andrews, 1985).

Congress has reinforced the role of the employer in the distribution of occupational welfare benefits through statuatory policy and special tax treatment. It is probably not surprising that Congress has encouraged employers to share the responsibility for welfare.

Historically, Americans have believed in the value of work. This commitment to the value of "honest labor" is one of the few shared values in the culture of the nation. This shared value has lent a cohesiveness to the American society in the same way that religion and political ideology have cemented other cultures (Ozawa, 1982).

The interest of government employers and private corporations in the protection of income in old age predates that of Congress. The City of New York established a pension fund for the City's policemen in 1857. This plan was the nation's first public pension fund to cover state or local government employees. Eighteen years later, in 1875, the American Express Company became the first company in the United States to establish a pension plan that was financed solely by the employer. In 1880, the Baltimore and Ohio Railroad became the first organization to sponsor a plan with contributions from both employer and employee.

Income security in retirement came to academia when in 1892 Columbia University pensioned its professors who had fifteen years of service. Chicago followed on the heels of Columbia University and pensioned public school teachers in 1893. In 1901 Carnegie Steel developed the first pension plan in the steel industry to endure. Not to be outdone, Standard Oil offered employee pensions in 1903. The Granite Cutters of America, in 1905, became the first union to actually pay pension benefits to its members. That same year the Carnegie Foundation for the Advancement of Teaching established the teachers' insurance plan for retirement income. Congress joined the act in 1920 by creating a fund to support Federal Civil Service Retirement and Disability. In 1921 Metropolitan Life Insurance Company broke new ground by offering the first group annuity contract in the United States (American Council of Life Insurance, 1985).

Private initiatives in the development of these income security plans were first supported by Congress with the Revenue Act of 1921. This Act gave tax exempt status to company-sponsored trusts that financed qualified profit-sharing or stock-option plans. Five years later with passage of the 1926 Revenue Act, trustees as well as the insurers of these trusts were given tax exempt status on the trust earnings. By 1950 there were two thousand pension funds in the United States (Drucker, 1976).

The next legislation to affect privately sponsored retirement plans was the monumental Internal Revenue Act of 1942. This act contained the first substantive national public policy considerations for democratizing the private pension plans. In order to qualify for tax exempt status after the 1942 Revenue Act the private sector was required to design pension plans that were non-discriminatory. This condition was defined by the Internal Revenue Service (IRS) as:

1. The plan must be for the exclusive benefit of employees and/or their beneficiaries.

2. The sole purpose of the trust must be to give employees a share of employer profits.

3. The plan must be permanent, in writing and communicated to the employees.

4. The plan must not discriminate in favor of officers, stockholders or the highly compensated.

In addition, the 1942 Act specified that employer contributions to a pension would not be taxed as current income to employees but would be taxed when received as income. This was the introduction of the tax advantages for deferred compensation in industry (King, 1978; Munnell, 1982).

In retrospect, the 1942 Act is considered limited in scope. However, it did serve to provide some national standards for retirement income plans. In addition, new tax incentives were offered to the private sector to encourage the further development of pension plans. In 1950, twenty-two percent of all workers participated in pension plans. By 1970 participation in private pensions plans had increased to forty-eight percent of the working population (Kolodrubetz, 1972).

In contrast to the plethora of pension legislation enacted in recent years, the only significant pieces of legislation to be enacted between 1942 and 1974, were the Taft-Hartly Act in 1947, and the Welfare and Pension Disclosure Act in 1958. The Taft-Hartly Act created the negotiated trusteeships between corporations and the unions. The courts ruled in the case of Inland Steel that employers of organized industries were required to negotiate pension benefits, placing them for the first time, within the union's "terms of agreement." The Welfare and Pension Disclosure Act in 1958, addressed financial abuses on the part of pension fund trustees. Amazing though it may seem, at no time prior to 1974 did the Internal Revenue Service indicate a concern for the financial soundness of the private pension plans. Nor did Congress express a concern for the rights of the participants to accrued assets (Kolokubetz, 1972).

Impact of the Private Sector

The Inland Steel case, by introducing pensions as a negotiable labor relations item, precipitated changes which were initiated by Charles Wilson, the chief executive officer of General Motors. Considered radical at the time, Wilson's 1950 proposal to the United Auto Workers changed the structure of the private pension funds in significant ways. Wilson proposed that pension investments no longer focus on annuities such as government bonds and mortgages.

These fixed and low-interst pension fund investments were rejected for capital-based equities. This placed pension funds in production resources rather than in government resources that had debt claims against them. This change from investment in government bonds and other annuities, to investment in the market through equities, made pension funds the business of the private sector. This created a greatly improved investment vehicle to support the financial liabilities of corporate promises for income security for retirees.

By default then, this structural change represented a much greater "expense", and new level of public financial support, via tax deferrals and exemptions, to Congress. In addition, before this, Congress was exempting from taxes what was largely the business of Congressional robbing-Peter-to-pay-Paul, so to speak. Also significant, the Wilson plan was contingent on the relinquishment of union control of the pension funds to the company, for management by independent assets managers (Drucker, 1976).

This gave pension funds, according to business, the potential of more reliable management by professionals in the business. It also changed the locus of control of large pools of money from the unions and the workers to the insurers and trustees of pension funds in the banking industry, reducing, by consolidation, the base of the income tax system. With this change of control, went the financially significant tax advantage on pension fund earnings to the trust sponsors, via the trust fiduciaries, consistent with the 1926 legislation.

Interestingly, it was found in 1985 that early estimates by the Securities and Exchange Commission (SEC) on pension trust fund assets on which Congress had based most information, were seriously underestimated. Belatedly, Congress has recognized the impact of the pools of pension funds on the banking and insurance markets, and the dynamic created by the tax revenue that is foregone (Andrews, 1985).

General Motors, acting without Congressional mandate, and most likely pre-empting Congressional understanding of the potential of trusts for manipulation and avarice, established four rules for good pension management. These rules were adopted by the majority of large employers and were also incorporated into the 1974 Employee Retirement Income Security Act. The four rules for employers to live by were that:

1.   Pension funds were to be professionally and flexibly managed, as investments under the administration of the corporation.

2.   There should be a minimal or better still, no investment in the employing corporation.

3. There should be no investment in any one company in excess
of five percent of the company's total capital.

4. There could be no more than ten percent of the fund's
total assets invested in the employing company.

In the opinion of Wilson, "Investing the worker's main savings in the
business that employs him may be 'industrial democracy' but it is
financial irresponsibility" (Drucker, 1976, p. 8). He saw such an
investment masquerading as a subsidy to the employing corporation, and
an unacceptable risk for employees.

Pension Reform

The 1974 Employee Retirement Income Security Act (ERISA),
commonly known as the Pension Reform Act, was signed into law by
President Ford on Labor Day, September 2, 1974. ERISA is recognized
as the most comprehensive employee benefits legislation ever enacted
in the United States. ERISA affects millions of workers who are
covered by private-sector income security plans. ERISA marked a new
stage in public policy regarding privately sponsored benefit plans.

With the passage of ERISA Congress mandated that employers who
made promises regarding deferred compensation must follow specific
procedures to ensure their financial capacity to meet those promises.
ERISA became the first in a series of bills that had a significant
effect on the shape and direction of employee benefits (Grubbs, 1985).

For the first time, statutory policy focused on the individual
participants in private pension plans, and their rights to accrued
employee benefits. For those employers offering qualified defined

benefit (pension) plans the mandatory age rule for participation by the employees was set at age twenty-five and one year of service.

Vesting schedules, which entitle the participant to a full share of the deferred compensation after a specified number of years with the corporation, were also established by the Internal Revenue Service. These vesting schedules then became part of the Internal Revenue Code (IRC). In addition, a corporate Simplified Plan Description detailing the employers' income security plan for retirees, that could be easily understood, became an annual requirement (SPD). With the passage of ERISA, employers were also required, for the first time, to file an annual deferred compensation report with the IRS.

ERISA also set limits on the contributions that employers and employees could make to deferred compensation plans. In addition, the trust fund fiduciaries, who administer pension plan investments, were now regulated and monitored by the IRS. ERISA set yet another precedent. Employees without pension coverage were given individual tax advantages for contributing to retirement income through Individual Retirement Accounts (P.L. 93-406). Now all members of the welfare state were awarded the opportunity of taking advantage of a tax incentive to develop an income security plan for retirement.

Prior to 1974, business failure often resulted in an employee losing accrued retirement income benefits. In response to this situation, Congress established a scheme of mandatory plan insurance for the private sector defined benefit plans. The Pension Benefit

Guarantee Corporation (PBGC) was established to administer plan
insurance. All employers with defined benefit (pension) plans were
now required to pay a premium of $2.50 per employee towards the
insurance of any and all private defined benefit plans.

The PBGC, a quasi-governmental corporation, is required under
the terms of the federal charter, to insure basic benefits to plan
participants. In cases of bankruptcy and termination of plans,
thirty percent of the defaulting corporation's assets are impounded by
the government to satisfy pension claims. Pension claims must be
honored ahead of any other employer liabilities. ERISA made the
termination of pension rights a detailed and public procedure, which
focuses on the rights of the participants.

The broad issue now facing the Congress is whether ERISA and
subsequent legislation designed to improve coverage, participation and
vesting will encourage the termination of plans, or will encourage
plan development by employers.

All tax expenditures are presently being questioned in
Congress, and attention has focused on the insurers and trustees of
large pension fund trusts. The impact of these large financial pools
on the national economy is being questioned. Levitan (1984) reports
that pension trusts represent the largest single pool of new investment capital in the nation. He suggests that the aim of Congress is
to limit the tax deferred status afforded employer-sponsored pensions
and trust fund income. However, it is these trusts and the tax
deferred status that have made it efficient for employers to

participate in the welfare state's plan for income security of the retiree.

Occupational welfare has flourished in an environment of strong economic growth and legislative encouragement. However, both the economy and the legislation have undergone significant change this past decade. These changes can be expected to impact this privately sponsored retirement income system.

The Decade after ERISA

Congressional hearings had waved the spectre of a mandatory private pension in front of "free enterprise" for more than a decade. ERISA, under the skillful direction of Senator Jacob Javits of New York, caught the corporate unified front napping. ERISA failed to establish a mandatory pension system, but did succeed in alerting the private sector that protection of their interests from the ravages of legislation called for their concerted attention.

The 1970s saw business greatly expand its activities in Washington in an effort to influence Congress and to keep its consti-tuency informed (Vogel, 1983). The word was, "You have zero chance of scoring points unless you get into the game" (Levitan and Cooper, 1984, p. 5). The Roundtable, made up of chief executive officers (CEOs) of major corporations, came to Washington in 1972, the National Association of Manufacturers arrived in 1974, the National Federation of Independent Business in 1975, and between 1981 and 1982 the Chamber of Commerce doubled its presence in Washington. By 1978 the pension industry and the private employers had developed what is now the best current source of data on the private income security system, the Employee Benefit Research Institute (EBRI). The EBRI systematically collects data to support positions the private sector feels it must champion. Reginald Jones, the former CEO of General Electric, said, "Public policy and social issues are no longer adjuncts to business planning and management. They are in the mainstream of it" (Levitan and Cooper, 1984, p. 53).

The years following ERISA were ones of private sector compliance and adjustment to the new all-encompassing standards legislated by the Act. By 1978 the private sector was responding to statutory and regulatory policy.

At a time when early retirement was accelerating, Congress passed the Age Discrimination in Employment Act Amendments in 1978 (ADEA). This Act raised the age when employers could force retirement from sixty-five to seventy years of age. This Act coincided with changes in the Social Security Act, phasing in the postponement of full Social Security benefits over a period of years, to age sixty-seven instead of sixty-five. By the year 2010 retirees will wait two additional years before becoming eligible for the public portion of their pensions.

For those private pension plans which are integrated with Social Security, and many are, this will mean early retirees must expect a smaller percentage of replacement income in retirement years prior to age sixty-seven. This also means that those employees who

retired early may not be able to live in the manner to which they have
become accustomed without other financial resources.

Interestingly enough, despite ADEA's seeming support for the
older worker, employers are allowed by statute, to exclude employees
hired after their fifty-ninth birthday from the qualified defined
benefit plans. This allows employers who base eligibility and
benefits on the last five years of employment to exclude newly hired
older workers from the company plans. Older workers are then offered
specially tailored income security plans, which might not have such a
high employer cost factor and conversely, such a high employee benefit
factor. Often, these "new hires" are "former employees" who had been
urged by income supplements to retire, then rehired on a new benefit
schedule. In the corporate vernacular, these employees are often
given the title of "consultant" to the company.

This suggests long-range cost containment by the employer of
future income security liabilities. It is significant that case law
has deemed that benefits received on retirement become a status right
and cannot be withdrawn or altered without the retiree's consent.
Prior to this challenge to the private sector, employers saw any
changes in benefits of their retirees as dependent on current benefits
management decisions, or union terms of agreement.

The Revenue Act (P.L. 95-600)

Up until 1978, and the passage of the Revenue Act, the focus
of Congress appeared to be on the private sector development of
qualified retirement plans for employees, to guarantee post-work

income security. However, the Revenue Act of 1978 set a new national precedent. For the first time, Congress used the system of tax exemptions to encourage employers as well as employees to save by offering the individual a tax incentive. History shows that a coalition of employers, supported with statistics from the fledging Employee Benefit Research Institute, challenged the planning commission's estimates on pension coverage, as too conservative. This implied that there was no need for Congress to mandate the employers to develop income security plans. These employers emphasized tax incentives to encourage savings as an alternative to a compulsory pension system. The results of this lobbying by business was the 401(k) (Levitan and Cooper, 1984).

Following the Revenue Act, Section 401(k) of the Internal Revenue Code allowed employers to establish a retirement savings plan to which employees could contribute tax-free dollars. These contributions were excluded from the employee's annual gross taxable income. The plan assets are not taxed until employees begin receiving them. The tax advantages offered by the 401(k) make it possible for the employee, at some critical point, to contribute before-tax dollars to a retirement savings plan, and still have the same take-home pay. In some cases the employee may even have more take-home pay.

Technically, even the lowest paid employee can now save for retirement with the help of the government, and the discretion of the employer, at no reduction in real income. Voluntary contributions by the employer, encouraged by an attractive tax treatement, and pre-tax

242

status for savings for the employee make salary deferrals for retirement an addition to earnings, rather than a reduction from present
salary. The non-discrimination rules which are imposed as a condition
of favorable tax treatment ensure that these advantages are equally
available to all of the employees of a given group.

The IRS standards require that a specific ratio be maintained
between the low-paid employees and the high-paid employees (Beam,
1985). The tax advantages of the 401(k) are so attractive, that
management is usually encouraged to actively promote participation
among low-level employees so that higher-level employees will have the
privilege of participation. It should be noted that organized labor's
stand against "contributory" retirement plans for workers has excluded
union members from participation in this national benefit which allows
employees to save before paying taxes.

In addition, the 1978 Revenue Act, Section 125, introduced the
concept of "cafeteria" plans for "funded welfare" and health benefits.
Employees were now able to take responsibility for making individual
choices about what benefits would best suit their needs, thus
supporting only those benefits relevant to their individual needs and
avoiding the cost of benefits which did not apply to their situation.
Pre-retirees have needs quite different from those employees who are
under forty-five years of age. This bill also allowed favorable tax
treatment for prepaid legal and educational services, as well as
dependent care credits. These benefits have financial implications
for employees planning for retirement. Now prospective retirees can

retrain for a new career, and get financial relief in the cost of the care of a dependent parent, spouse or child, through the system of tax exemptions.

The dollars that the employer allows for benefits can be individually tailored to focus on the pre- and post-retirement needs. This realizes a social "savings" in those benefit areas which are of no interest to an individual employee.

It is interesting that in 1981 the Internal Revenue Service should finally issue guidelines for Chapter 852 of the 1928 Revenue Act! The IRC 501(C)(9), now clarified, allows employers to establish "Voluntary Employee Benefit Associations" (VEBAs) for the pre-funding of "funded welfare". That is, benefits such as life, disability and major medical insurance, severance pay, vacation pay, educational benefits, job readjustment allowances, income maintenance payments in the event of economic dislocation, loans and grants in the event of disaster and group legal services can be established (Sweeney, 1984).

Benefits under a VEBA, as defined by IRC 501(c)(9), are intended to safeguard or improve a member's health or protect him/her against an event which might interrupt or impair earning power, are financed by tax credits rather than tax deductions. This is finan- cially significant to the employer because it avoids the corporate tax rate penalty. This means that one hundred percent of the corporate dollar is regained. In addition, premiums are excluded from Social Security and the unemployment tax. VEBAs are governed under "ordinary, necessary and reasonable" rules of the IRC Section 162,

244

rather than the qualified pension and profit-sharing restrictions of IRC, Sections 405 and 415. This gives employers considerable discretion in designing affordable benefit plans. VEBAs offer employers and employees cost benefits through the tax system, in the form of "funded welfare" benefit packages, often available to retirees, at the lowest possible cost (Sweeney, 1984). The 401(k)s and VEBAs represent cost efficient and socially effective means of enhancing retirement income security.

The Economic Recovery Tax Act (ERTA) (P.L. 97-34, 1981)

ERTA, heralded by Congress as a restructuring of the entire tax system, also emphasized savings in employee benefit plans. ERTA allowed already pensioned employees an additional tax credit of two thousand dollars annually to buy Individual Retirement Accounts. The Tax Reform Act of 1986 has since limited this benefit by annual income. Older employees are more likely than younger employees to have discretionary income to invest and save in this way. With this in mind, the pre-retirees can be considered the Congressional target group and the primary beneficiary (Shidler and Cziok, 1981).

In addition, ERTA offered tax incentives to encourage the growth of Employee Stock Option Plans (ESOPS) and Payroll Stock Options (PAYSOPS). PAYSOPS are often referred to by benefits managers as the "closest thing to a free lunch around." PAYSOPS allowed employers a tax credit for a contribution of employer stock to their employees in place of pay, costing both employer and employee nothing.

In addition, both the employer and the employee escape payroll taxes which result in additional real income. PAYSOPS serve to encourage both the employers and the employees to save via investment in the company. PAYSOPS were designed by Congress, as part of the focus on the economy of the Economic Recovery Act. PAYSOPS were intended to encourage a new level of employee motivation and participation, by way of personal interest in the company's stock value.

The Tax Equity and Fiscal Responsibility Act (TEFRA) (P.L. 97-248)

The years of 1978 and 1981 have been referred to as the years of "rational benefit planning," maybe because the business community, in escaping mandatory pensions, and encouraging a focus on savings, felt they had wielded some influence (Mercer, 1984). This era came to a quick halt with the Tax Equity and Fiscal Responsibility Act of 1982. Setting a new precedent, TEFRA allowed limited or complete taxation of private pension plans. In addition, TEFRA made more changes in the law affecting qualified retirement plans than any act since the passage of ERISA in 1974. According to Facciani (1984), Congress now planned a major assault on the favorable tax advantages of private pension plans. In his estimation, the Treasury grossly overestimated the tax losses associated with retirement plans, and suggested that the private pension trust funds offer an inviting target to Congress for offsetting current and future budget deficits. The concern of Congress now, according to Facciani, is predicated on budget issues, whereas prior to TEFRA the concern of Congress was predicated on social issues. Facciani fails to consider the issue of the dynamic impact of "tax expense" funds on the banking and insurance industries and thus the national economy.

TEFRA placed restrictions on the maximum dollar limitations for qualified contribution plans and qualified benefit plans. The level for integration with Social Security was lowered, which limited the "redress" that higher-paid employees could anticipate from this progressive approach to taxation. TEFRA identified and regulated "top-heavy" plans, that is, those retirement plans where key employees accumulate sixty percent or more of the contributions or benefits under the plan.

After TEFRA, top-heavy plans were required to specify one of two vesting schedules and meet minimum benefit or minimum contribution requirements. TEFRA also required that top-heavy plans provide a minimum of benefits and/or contributions to non-key employees as well. For instance, the employer's share cannot be less than three percent of all employee's compensation. The absolute dollar limits allowed key employees in defined contribution plans changed from $90,000 to $30,000. For defined benefit plans, the absolute dollar limit was reduced from $136,425 to $90,000. Now too, the full amount of the retirement plan coverage, less the employee's contribution, is con-sidered taxable income. This effectively undermines nonqualified benefits as a prerequisite for key employees. In addition, TEFRA, consistent with the Old Age Discrimination in Employment Act, required that employers offer the same health benefits to employees aged sixty-five to sixty-nine as are offered to younger employees.

The Deficit Reduction Act (DEFRA)
(P.L. 97-248)

DEFRA followed closely on the heels of TEFRA, in 1984. DEFRA introduced a plethora of complex rules to regulate "funded welfare". Funded welfare refers to the prepayment of life, disability and health insurance, and other benefits which employees and retirees enjoy. The practice in the private sector of developing trust funds to self-pay health care costs has now become a potential tax liability. Tax-free funds in these trusts are now limited by DEFRA to ten percent over the estimated liability. Any funds in excess of this ten percent are taxed as "unrelated business income" (Footer, 1985). DEFRA appears to reverse the position of Congress which has historically supported private sector benefits expansion of funded welfare.

Concomitant with DEFRA the Financial Accounting Standards Board in 1984 began requiring that post-work medical benefits costs become a footnote to financial statements. The rationale for this was that senior managers would have a heightened awareness of the employer costs of these benefits.

While restricting the growth of funded welfare benefits, DEFRA regulations encouraged growth of the Employee Stock Option Plans, which is seen as a "savings" or "conservation" factor in the scheme of retirement income security (Spector, 1984). This investment in the employer's company, however, was seen by General Motors Charles Wilson as "financial irresponsibility."

The Retirement Equity Act (REA)

In 1984, the Retirement Equity Act became the fifth piece of major legislation on employee benefits in seven years. REA expanded the standards of plan participation so that employees age twenty-one would begin earning retirement benefits. Vesting became five years or less, and new rules were promulgated regarding survivor benefits. With broad implications for women, and sometimes hostile and critical reception in the business community, REA authorizes but does not require, courts to treat spouse's pensions as an asset of marriage, to be distributed at normal retirement age. In addition, survivor benefits can be awarded to parties involved in divorce. REA makes survivor benefits automatic should the worker die and the spouse survive. The removal of a spouse as a pension beneficiary now requires written and notarized permission from the party involved.

Consistent with what appears to be the Congressional interest in the individual's control of his retirement security and undermining the control of pension trusts, REA requires that plan administrators notify pre-retirees that distribution of pension assets are eligible for roll-over into an IRA or other qualified plans. Failure to do so carries a five thousand dollar fine. In addition, retirees are advised that benefits received in a lump sum are eligible for a ten-year income averaging treatment to ameliorate the tax burden

(P.L. 98-397). This represents a significant tax advantage to the retiree (Beam and McFadden, 1985).

The Consolidated Omnibus Budget Reconciliation Act (COBRA) (P.L. 97-272)

The most recent piece of legislation affecting health benefits for employees may have implications for retirees and their families. The Consolidated Omnibus Budget Reconciliation Act of 1985 requires that employers allow terminated employees to elect coverage under the group health plan for themselves and/or their families for eighteen to thirty-six months, depending on the circumstance. In a sense this bill redefines the meaning of the term employee, extending it beyond active employment. In addition, medical costs for the unemployed are shifted to either the employer or the group of employees, depending on the plan, from the public sector. In those situations where employees have not continued benefits for active employees into retirement, COBRA may represent precedent-setting legislation. COBRA imposes additional responsibility on the market sector for the welfare of employees, both active and inactive. This legislation, coupled with the court's recognition of the "status" benefits already guaranteed for retirees, could serve to curtail corporate benefit planning in the name of caution and concern for future cost. Employers, since DEFRA, cannot prefund these extensive benefits without a tax penalty.

250

Conclusion

In the past ten years Congress has passed legislation which has significantly shaped the corporate approach to retirement security planning for their employees. Minimum standards for participation have been established, vesting schedules and survivor benefits have been delineated. The minimum funding requirements have strengthened benefit security in those plans which were underfunded.

Predictably, the public and private sector costs for pension plan terminations have soared. The original 1974 premium of $2.50 has risen to $8.50 per employee participant, effectively inhibiting the employer's enthusiasm for defined benefit plans. This has become especially true since the profitable corporation pays a price for the corporation which is not well run.

An historical perspective shows that in 1960, thirty-five percent of the population over sixty-five was in poverty. By 1979 only fifteen percent of those over sixty-five were in poverty. This is seen as a result of both public and private programs for income security. The 1935 Social Security Act guaranteed a floor of income security to the nation's retirees. With the passage of ERISA the Congress recognized and actively encouraged the role and the responsibility of the private sector in retirement income planning. Employees who were promised pensions now have had them guaranteed by statutory policy. Concomitantly, statutory policy has encouraged employers to develop health and welfare packages which extend into retirement (U.S. Congress, House, Select Committee on Aging, 1987).

The bad news for employees is that employers are under no obligation to offer retirement income plans. In addition, employers can terminate pension plans at their discretion, unless these plans are terms of a union agreement. The good news is that once retired, accrued pension benefits are inviolate.

Having shaped the direction and the nature of the private pension system, Congress focussed on the question of the third leg of income security, that is, savings. Scholars such as Munnell (1982) see Social Security as having inhibited the American worker's perception of a need to have personal savings for retirement.

The trend of recent legislation suggests that Congress is now encouraging employer and employee interest in individual savings by way of the qualified contribution plans with irresistable tax advantages. Coupled with these tax incentives are the recent employer disincentives for development of defined benefit plans. These disincentives are in the form of regulations which threaten the employer's financial incentives for creating pension trusts, frequent statutory changes and excessive regulation by the IRS, unwelcome administrative burdens for employers, and the rapid increase in PBGC premiums.

The corporate pension system is adversely affected by inflation from the perspective of the already retired, but not from the perspective of the trust. The security attributed to a future set income for a retiree is beginning to be seen as illusionary. The apparent trend away from statutory encouragement of defined pensions to the encouragement of defined contributions appears to be a trend which will discourage corporate paternalism and encourage the portability of retirement benefits between places of employment.

Beam and McFadden (1985) report a sprinkling of "hybrid" plans, that is, those plans which combine both defined benefit and defined contribution retirement plans. This suggests an assumption of mutual responsibility in the planning for retirement between employer and employee. Such plans will allow an employee to be more mobile and also will allow increased protection during times of inflation/market failure. The defined contribution plans appear to be consistent with the concept of investment-based economic growth as exemplified by ERTA.

It is being suggested that the fourth leg to the retirement security stool is necessary for optimum stability. A part of that fourth leg is seen as coming from income derived from the new careers in which retirees will be involved. It is anticipated that this will broaden the Social Security base and is consistent with the new retirement age of sixty-seven. The trend for the American worker has been towards early retirement from "career service." Many of these early retirees are expected to seek new careers. It can be anticipated that a good number will be stimulated to seek new careers by the tax advantages offered for individual saving for retirement. This will shelter discretionary income from taxation. In addition, early retirement from income-producing work becomes less attractive as Social Security benefits are delayed and private benefits are taxed.

From the perspective of the Congress, every employee payroll deduction helps improve the slim margin maintained by the Social Security Trust. The nation's retirement programs are being threatened both by changes in the demographics of the nations, and the claims against the Pension Benefit Guarantee Corporation.

The Congress appears to have a vested interest in keeping the employee in the workforce, recognizing marriage as an economic unit, and increasing the role of individuals in their future economic security. In part, these interests have been served by supporting the claims of women to the benefits of working spouses. In a very short time this focus will benefit from an androgenous interpretation of financial support for each member of the economic unit formed through marriage.

The interest of the welfare state has been served by the attractive tax incentives which focus on individual savings and work. The assumption is that employees will always be tempted to feather their retirement nest as nicely as possible, and that employers will welcome a reduction in future economic responsibility for retirees.

The question the social policy analyst must ask is whether or not the interests of Congress and the interest of the citizens of the welfare state are congruent. Has Congress legislated changes which increase the employees' opportunities for retirement security while also assuring equality of access to those opportunities? Has Congress served universal interests of retirees by focusing on the third leg of income security seen as individual savings? Is Congressional interest congruent with the citizens' interest when national policy hints that a fourth leg to the income security stool might be paid work for those past normal retirement age? Given the number of citizens happily retired today, this seems a rather tenuous leg on which to rest national policy for income security of the aged.

Should Congress develop national retirement income security policies for citizens of the welfare state based on employment, if employers can choose whether or not employees should have access to tax-advantaged programs? Should Congress develop national welfare policy based on employment relationships without full employment policies or when employers cannot be held accountable for the income security of their retirees?

Congressional legislation appears to be shifting the responsibility for retirement security from the "national community" and "collectivism" implied by Roosevelt and the 1935 Social Security Act, to the individual employee through added years of work and regular reductions in discretionary income. Within the framework of a modern welfare state which assumes responsibility for promoting and guarding the welfare of the whole community, cost effectiveness must be in balance with the social effectiveness of welfare policy (Marshall, 1965).

The American welfare state seems to reflect the concept of equifinality from General System Theory by recognizing that "there is more than one way to skin a cat" in the achievement of the national goal of economic security in old age. However, without careful attention to the propositions of integration, on which equifinality is based, Congressional initiatives to promote private income security may fail those citizens most in need of economic protection.

The American welfare state was seen by Titmuss as unique and limited in that benefits of the state are based on a citizen's relationship to the market. As a consequence, the patterned measures of a citizen's eligibility for benefits are status, associated with wealth and merit, associated with employment, in conjunction with need which is associated with dependency.

For those working citizens whose employers do not give access to retirement plans, who have poor jobs and less discretionary income, this trend toward increasing the employee's responsibility for income protection in old age might further accentuate the observed inequities of the American social welfare system.

Table 6 illustrates the impact of these Congressional acts on the corporations of this study.

256

TABLE 6

IMPACT OF ACTS OF CONGRESS ON STUDY CORPORATIONS

Acts of Congress	Impact on Corporations

Tax Incentives for Defined Contribution Plans:
1978 Revenue Act: 401(k)
  employee tax incentives
  to save
1981 ERTA: PAYSOPs
  tax credits to employees
  to encourage profit-sharing
	Corporate Adoption of Defined Contribution Plans:
	1982-1985 401(k)
	  Cray Research, Dayton Hudson, General Mills,
	  Honeywell, 3M, Pillsbury, Super Valu, Toro
	1982 PAYSOPs
	  Dayton Hudson, General Mills, Honeywell, 3M,
	  Pillsbury, Toro, Super Valu

Tax Disincentives for Defined Benefits Plans:
1982 TEFRA: Limited integration of
  of defined benefit with
  Social Insurance, limited
  tax-deferred perquisites,
  increased corporate costs
1984 DEFRA: Limited tax-free funding
  of welfare trusts, limited
  control of fiduciary
  over excess assets in
  pension trusts, increased
  corporate costs
1984 REA: Expanded employee partici-
  pation in defined benefit
  plans, expanded eligibility
  for pension benefits to
  employees and also depen-
  dents, increased corporate
  costs.
	Change in Corporate Focus:
	1985 From Defined Benefit Plan to
	  Defined Contribution Plan
	  Dayton Hudson, General Mills, Honeywell, 3M,
	  Pillsbury, Toro, Super Valu
	1985 Change in Relationship of Defined Benefit
	  Plan to Defined Contribution Plan
	  Dayton Hudson, General Mills, Pillsbury

APPENDIX B

IMPACT OF TAX INCENTIVES ON THE
CORPORATE INCOME SECURITY PLANNING

TAX APPROPRIATION AND TAX EXPENSE SYSTEMS
MODELS OF KEYNESIAN AND POST-KEYNESIAN ECONOMICS

TAX APPROPRIATIONS: Represents scarce resources as a 'pie' which must be divided to meet the economic/social needs of the state. One must increase appropriations in order to increase the size of the pie.

Appropriations focus on the product and assume that prediction and prescription are both possible and desirable. The method is analytic and reductionist and has little congruence with the social work interest in 'process' but does address dependency and the security needs of society identified as problematic.

'The Pie,' the Keynesian system of appropriations: for meeting social needs through the redistribution of tax appropriations by dividing up these limited resources between competing needs. A REACTIVE METHOD of redistribution to meet social needs.

The Post-Keynesian, tax-expense system: The 'Baker's Model' represents the yeast which is used in making bread to control the size/output of the loaf. With a little more yeast, or temperature change, among other options, one can end up with a much bigger loaf and very little 'real expenditure.'

Tax incentives assume that events are synergistic and based on an historical and evolutionary process. The method is evaluation and includes both fact and value. Post-Keynesian principles are congruent with the social work strengths' perspective, interest in 'process' and prevention, empowerment of people, and the ecology of situations. Equity and adequacy in redistribution are problematic.

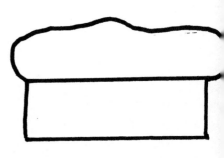

BREAD-creating a 'social surplus' by adding ingredients and adjusting the environment. A PROACTIVE METHOD of redistribution to meet social needs.

APPENDIX C

LETTERS

260

 UNIVERSITY OF MINNESOTA
TWIN CITIES

School of Social Work
400 Ford Hall
224 Church Street S.E.
Minneapolis, Minnesota 55455

(612) 624-5888

June 3, 1986

Mr. Fred Hamacher, Vice President
Compensation and Benefits
Dayton Hudson, Incorporated
700 Nicollet Mall
Minneapolis, MN 55402

Dear Mr. Hamacher:

Thank you so much for agreeing to meet with me on June 6 at 10:00 am.

Attached is a synopsis of the research project on corporate pensions.
It will give you a skeleton idea of the study as well as information
on how I can be reached if necessary.

Please feel free to contact my advisor if you would like additional
information. Professor George Hoshino can reached reached at his
office in the School of Social Work, University of Minnesota (612/
373-2649).

I am looking forward to meeting with you on Friday.

Sincerely,

Ruth Y. Winger

UNIVERSITY OF MINNESOTA
TWIN CITIES

School of Social Work
400 Ford Hall
224 Church Street S.E.
Minneapolis, Minnesota 55455

(612) 624-5888

PROJECT SYNOPSIS

Title of Project

A Preliminary Exploration of the Impact of Tax Legislation on Corporate Income Security Programs for Retirees.

Researcher

Ruth Y. Winger, Doctoral Candidate, School of Social Work, University of Minnesota, 400 Ford Hall, Minneapolis, MN 55455, 612/370-0311 (home) or 612/624-0374 (office).

Purpose

The income security of the growing population of retired persons (now at 11.2%) will have an increasing impact on the national social and economic well-being. Despite the expansion in scope and coverage of public income security programs over the last 50 years, private income provisions remain fundamental to income protection of Americans. An understanding of the impact of federal tax legislation on corporate retirement policies is germane to the policy analysts concerned with the universal income security needs of retirees.

The Research Project

This research will examine the impact of tax incentives on corporate pension plans for retirees from 1975-1985. Nine corporations that are willing to work with the researcher in identifying the trends in pension planning between 1975 and 1985 will make up the sample for this study.

The history of tax legislation and Internal Revenue Service codes and regulations will be examined in relation to corporate pension policies in a ten-year period. It is anticipated that corporate policy will reflect the changes in tax laws. Other factors that have influenced corporate policy on retiree pensions also will be taken into account.

262

Semi-structured interviews will be conducted with the corporate chief
executive or the designated representative of each corporation. It
is hoped that corporations will submit copies of their IRS Form 5200,
"Summary of Plan Decription" for the years 1978 and 1985 for data
purposes. Permission to tape the interview will be sought (but not
required) to strengthen the reliability of the questionnaire results.

This research proposal is on file with the University of Minnesota
Committee on the Use of Human Subjects in Research (612/373-9895).

College of Saint Benedict
37 South College Avenue
St. Joseph, MN 56374-2099

August 14, 1986

Mr. Allen Richie
Corporate Director
Compensation and Employee Benefits
General Mills
P.O. Box 1113
Minneapolis, MN 55440

Dear Mr. Richie:

Once again, thank you for the time that you spent with me yesterday.

I appreciate your willingness to send me copies of your IRS 5500s for
the defined benefit and defined contribution plans of 1984 and 1978.
Also the Summary of Plan Description and the company's annual report.
These will all serve to keep me honest!

Hopefully, I will have this study completed before spring. I will
see that you get an executive summary. No doubt I will have questions
that need expert answers before that time. I appreciate your willingness to help.

Sincerely,

Ruth Y. Winger

Address after August 27:

College of St. Benedict
St. Joseph, MN 56374
612/363-5384

Honeywell

July 30, 1986

Ruth Y. Winger
University of Minnesota
School of Social Work
400 Ford Hall
224 Church Street S.E.
Minneapolis, MN 55455

Subject: BENEFIT RESEARCH PROJECT

-- rather than provide a rambling narrative to the PAYSOP
questions, I have enclosed a descriptive brochure from 1982 and
a current SPD which will perhaps provide more than you requested
with regard to PAYSOPS.

... in reply to Question 8: This is a strong position, but I
maintain the benefit is an entitlement - a concept which seems
to have emerged following World War II. It is relatively little
different from the employer providing a safe place to work,
necessary tools/training to do a job, etc. - added justification
is that the <u>funding</u> of the <u>entitlement</u> is part of the cost of
the goods/services sold by the employer.

Howard H. Amborn
Pension/Retirement Department

HHA/js
Enclosures

APPENDIX D

QUESTIONNAIRE

Retirement income security is generally seen to be a combination of Social Security, pensions and individual savings.

This study looks at the design for income security for retirees in nine corporations. Of major interest is the role of federal tax incentives in the form of subsidies, credits and tax deferrals in the shaping of corporate retirement policy.

Introduction

1. In a market economy work and wages are of primary importance for general well-being. How do you, personally, feel the market can help meet the needs of people who do not have wages?

2. Can you describe to me how this corporation feels about its retired workers?

3. Do you see economic and social well-being of the nation's employees as two separate issues?

4. Who in this corporation is responsible for the design of the corporate retirement plans?

5. Who authorizes the cost to the company?

Corporate Policy

Two types of plans form the cornerstone of corporate post-work income security: (a) the qualified defined benefit plan which defers compensation and guarantees a certain income to retirees; and (b) the qualified defined contribution plans which individual deferred compensation accounts for each employee but in most cases do not guarantee any particular benefit.

6. Does your corporation offer

    a. a qualified defined benefit plan?
    b. a qualified defined contribution plan?
    c. a combination of both?
    d. a nonqualified benefit plan?
    e. a nonqualified contribution plan?

7. Who is eligible to participate in a qualified benefit plan?

    ____Age
    ____Service
    ____% Employer contribution
    ____% Employee contribution
    ____Plan formula
    ____Vesting
    ____Full vesting requirements

8. Would you consider a defined benefit plan an employee entitlement?

9. Who is eligible to participate in the qualified contribution plan?

    ____% Employer contribution
    ____% Employee contribution
    ____Plan formula
    ____Vesting type
    ____Full vesting requirements

10. Are your plans integrated? Which integration formula do you use? Why have you chosen this formula?

    a. separate
    b. off-set
    c. excess
    d. step-rate

11. In your opinion which retirement plan, defined benefit or defined contribution, gives the employer the "biggest bang for the buck"?

12. Do you see integration as a tool that will help control corporate pension costs? Has your integration formula changed since 1980? Would integrating the defined contribution plans more fully with the benefit and pay picture serve to save additional corporate tax revenue?

13. Your company makes a substantial contribution to Social Security through payroll taxes. Do you personally view Social Security as a means for

      a. redistributing income from people who are working now to people who will retire in the future?
      b. or as redistributing income from people who are working now to people who are now retired?

14. Do you see integration as a way to

      a. encourage private sector retirement plans?
      b. subsidize to produce general social goals?
      c. shelter tax?
      d. all of the above?
      e. Why should the Federal Government encourage integration?

Vesting

15. Five-year vesting is being considered. Will this have an impact on your corporation's retirement plans? In what way?

16. The reversion of pension trust fund assets is a current topic of discussion. When would you consider the reversion of trust fund assets justified? Why do you say that?

17. If you were to look at trust fund assets in terms of "ownership" who, in your opinion, is the owner of those funds?

Benefits

18. Corporations have played an important part in the income security of retirees. How would you rate the following incentives by order of importance to corporate decisions about retirement plans?

      a. human relations factor
      b. social responsibility
      c. union terms of agreement
      d. favorable federal tax treatment
      e. competitive position of the corporation

Most corporations offer qualified defined benefit plans to their employees as their primary retirement resource. However, options for qualified contributory plans have been increasing. What do you make of this?

19. In your corporation has the role of the qualified contribution plan for retirement changed in recent years? When did they change? How did they change?

20. Which of the following features are characteristic of your contribution plans?

a. loan features
b. hardship clause for withdrawal
c. reciprocity with other plans within the corporation and between corporations

21. Qualified defined contribution plans have many variations. Which of the following plans do you offer your employees?

a. Money-purchase pension plan

1) Why?
2) What is the formula?
3) Who participates or is eligible to participate?
4) When did you adopt the plan?
5) Is the plan qualified/nonqualified?
6) Is the plan integrated?
7) What is the vesting requirement?
8) When is the employee fully vested?

b. Profit-sharing plan

1) Why?
2) What is the formula?
3) Who participates or is eligible to participate?
4) When did you adopt the plan?
5) Is the plan qualified/nonqualified?
6) Is the plan integrated?
7) What is the vesting requirement?
8) When is the employee fully vested?

c. PAYSOP (Payroll Stock Option)

1) Why?
2) Who participates in the plan?
3) What are the vesting requirements?
4) When is the employee fully vested?

d. Section 401(k) plan

1) Why?
2) What is the formula?
3) Who participates or is eligible to participate?
4) When did you adopt the plan?
5) Is the plan qualified/nonqualified?
6) Is the plan integrated?
7) What is the vesting requirement?
8) When is the employee fully vested?
9) Does the plan have a loan feature?
10) Would you say that employees who participate have 100% of their dollar working for them in a 401(k)?

e. Stock-bonus plan

1) Why?
2) What is the formula?
3) Who participates or is eligible to participate?
4) When did you adopt the plan?
5) Is the plan qualified/nonqualified?
6) Is the plan integrated?
7) What is the vesting requirement?
8) When is the employee fully vested?

f. ESOP (Employee Stock Ownership Plan)

1) Why?
2) What is the formula?
3) Who participates or is eligible to participate?
4) When did you adopt the plan?
5) Is the plan qualified/nonqualified?
6) Is the plan integrated?
7) What is the vesting requirement?
8) When is the employee fully vested?

g. Incentive Stock Option Plans

1) Why?
2) What is the formula?
3) Who participates or is eligible to participate?
4) When did you adopt the plan?
5) Is the plan qualified/nonqualified?
6) Is the plan integrated?
7) What is the vesting requirement?
8) When is the employee fully vested?

271.

h. Employer-sponsored IRAs

    1) Why?
    2) Who participates or is eligible to participate?
    3) When did you adopt the plan?
    4) Does the corporation make a contribution? If so,
how much?

22. The three-legged stool of retirement income security is
considered to be Social Security, pensions and savings. Where will
the corporations place their emphasis in the next decade? Where do
you think the Congress is placing their emphasis at this time?

Administration

23. The defined benefit/contribution is

    a. trusteed, bank-administered
    b. trusteed, self-administered
    c. insured, group annuity
    d. insured, deposit-administered
    e. other

24. What is your current trust fund growth assumption?_____%
Does this represent a change? Since when? Why?

25. How are your trustees selected?

26. Who has the ultimate responsibility for investments?

27. Who has the responsibility for the administration of
these plans on a day-to-day basis?

28. Who is responsible for the overall design of the corporate
retirement plan?

    a. CEO
    b. Board of Directors
    c. Management____Department____
    d. Employees

29. Who authorizes the corporate cost of retirement plans? Do
you see these "costs" as deferred wages?

30. Has the Retirement Equity Act impacted your plans to a
significant degree? How has it made a difference? Has TEFRA made
benefits more expensive for your corporation? In what way?

31. As you have worked in this area, have you seen a shift in where the corporate emphasis has been placed? In what way has it changed?

Retirement

32. Normal retirement age_____service_____.

33. Early retirement age_____service_____.

34. Compensation formula.

35. Do you offer a supplement to retirees until they are eligible for Social Security?

36. How old are your current policies on early retirement? Have your policies changed since 1982, and why?

37. Do you offer pre-retirement counseling? Who is eligible? Do you focus on the individual or on groups of employees? What percentage of retirees opt for a lump-sum distribution of their deferred compensation?

38. Do you offer financial and investment planning to your employees? If so, when did you begin this? Who is eligible? In-house or outside consultant?

39. COBRA 2 has redefined "employee" to mean someone who no longer works for the corporation. How do you feel about this? Do you think this redefinition has future implications for the term retiree?

40. The indexing of pension plans has been repeatedly deferred. How has this affected your retirement income planning for the higher paid employees?

41. In your opinion does this act as a disincentive for qualified retirement plans? In what way?

42. Are the costs associated with the PBGC a significant factor in decisions regarding the choice between defined benefit and defined contributory plans?

43. Does a trade-off between PBGC costs which are associated with predictable future income, and employee participation in qualified contribution plans with a feature of unpredictability, seem acceptable? Why do you say that?

44. In your opinion are corporations moving from "managing benefits" to "managing the costs of benefits"?

45. As you have worked in this area, have you seen a shift in the locus of responsibility for post-work income security plans? In what way?

46. Will the benefits history of your corporation, and its implied expectations, conflict with the changing social and employment patterns of workers within which benefits operate?

Demographics

Corporation: Industrial group: Union:

Publically owned?   Number of employees

Average age of   Average years of
employee_____   service_____

Male/female ration: Employee groups:

                            a. Supplemental
                            b. Hourly production
                            c. Salaried

Normal retirement   Early retirement
age_____   age_____

Percent early   Incentives?
retirement_____

Corporate Tax   Responsibility?
Department?

Respondent

Title:

Rough age: <35   >35 but <45   >45 but <55   >55

Years of service at present corporation:

Previous experience:

Credentials:

SELECTED BIBLIOGRAPHY

Abramovitz, Mimi. "Everyone Is on Welfare: The Role of Distribution in Social Policy Revisited." Social Work 28 (November-December 1983): 440-445.

American Council of Life Insurance. "Pension Facts, 1982." In Employee Benefits, pp. 7, 96. By Burton T. Beam, Jr. and John G. McFadden. Homewood, Illinois: Richard D. Irwin, Inc., 1985.

Andrews, Emily S. The Changing Profile of Pensions in America. Washington, D.C.: Employee Benefit Research Institute, 1985.

Babbie, Earl R. The Practice of Social Research. Belmont, California: Wadsworth Publishing Co., Inc., 1975.

Baltzell, C. The Standardized Case Study: A Hybrid Approach to the Qualitative/Quantitative Issue. Presented at the Meeting of the American Educational Research Association, 1980.

Beam, Burton T., Jr. and John G. McFadden. Employee Benefits. Homewood, Illinois: Richard D. Irwin, Inc., 1985.

von Bertalanffy, Ludwig. General Systems Theory: Foundations, Development, Applications. New York: George Braziller, 1968.

_____. Perspectives on General Systems Theory. Edited by Edgar Tasholjian. New York: George Braziller, 1975.

_____. A Systems View of Man. Edited by Paul A. LaViolette. Boulder, Colorado: Westview Press, 1981.

Burns, Evaline M. Social Security and Public Policy. New York: McGraw-Hill, 1956.

Business Roundtable. Statement of the Retirement Income Policy Positions of the Business Roundtable. Washington, D.C.: The Business Rountable, 1981.

Campbell, Donald T. Foreword to Case Study Research: Design and Method by Robert K. Yin. Beverly Hills, California: Sage Publications, 1984.

Carter, Gene. "Private Pensions: 1982 Legislation." Social Security Bulletin 46, no. 2 (August 1983): 3-8.

274

Chambers, D. E. Social Policy and Social Programs: A Method for the Practical Public Policy Analyst. New York: Macmillan Publishing Co., 1986.

Checkland, Peter. Systems Thinking, Systems Practice. New York: John Wiley & Sons, 1981.

Coleman, James S. Policy Research in the Social Services. General Learning Corporation, 1972.

Congressional Budget Office. The Dislocated Workers: Issues and Federal Options. Washington, D.C.: Government Printing Office, 1982.

_____. Tax Expenditures: Current Issues and Five-Year Budget Projections for Fiscal Years 1982-1986. Washington, D.C.: U.S. Government Printing Office, 1982.

_____. Tax Expenditures: Budget Control Options and Five-Year Budget Projections for Fiscal Years 1984-1988. Washington, D.C.: U.S. Government Printing Office, 1982.

Cronbach, Lee J. Toward Reform of Program Evaluation. San Francisco: Jossey-Bass, 1980.

_____ and P. E. Meehl. "Construct Validity in Psychological Tests." Psychological Bulletin 52, no. 4: 281-302.

Davis, Lance E. and Douglass C. North. Institutional Change and American Economic Growth. New York: Cambridge University Press, 1971.

Devine, Joel A. and William Canak. "Redistribution in a Bifurcated Welfare State: Quartile Shares and the U.S. Case." Social Problems 33, no. 5 (June 1987): 391-404.

Drucker, Peter F. The Unseen Revolution. New York: Harper & Row, 1976.

Eccles, Sir John and Daniel M. Robinson. The Wonder of Being Human: Our Brain and Our Mind. New York: Collier Macmillan Publishers, 1984.

Eichner, Alfred S. "A Look Ahead." In A Guide to Post-Keynesian Economics (pp. 165-184). White Plains, New York: M. E. Sharpe, Inc., 1979.

Facciani, Gerald D. "Perspectives on National Pension Policy." Journal of Pension Planning and Compliance 10, no. 1 (February 1984): 5-11.

276

Firestone, William A. and Robert E. Herriott. "The Formalization of Qualitative Research." Evaluation Review (August 1983): 437-467.

Footer, Michael. "Funded Welfare Plans." Journal of Pension Planning and Compliance 11, no. 3 (Fall 1985): 225.

Geroch, Robert. General Relativity from A to B. Chicago: University of Chicago Press, 1978.

Gilbert, Neil. Capitalism and the Welfare State. New Haven: Yale University Press, 1983.

_____. "The Transformation of the Social Services." Social Service Review 51 (December 1977): 624-641.

_____. "The Welfare State Adrift." Social Work 31, no. 4 (1986).

_____ and Harry Specht. Dimensions of Social Welfare Policy. Englewood Cliffs, New Jersey: Prentice-Hall, Inc., 1974.

Glaser, Barney G. and Anselm L. Strauss. The Discovery of Grounded Theory: Strategies for Qualitative Research, 1967.

Grubbs, Donald S. "The Employee Retirement Income Security Act: The First Decade." Journal of Pension Planning and Compliance 11, no. 1 (Spring 1985): 44.

Hacker, Andrew. "Welfare: The Future of an Illusion." New York Times Book Review 32 (28 February 1985): 36-39.

Hoshino, George. "Social Services: The Problem of Accountability." In Social Administration. Edited by Simon Slavin, 1985.

Kettner, Peter M., John M. Daley and Ann Weaver Nichols. Initiating Change in Organizations and Communities. Monterey, California: Brooks/Cole Publishing Company, 1985.

King, Francis P. "The Future of Private and Public Employee Pensions." In Aging and Income: Programs and Prospects for the Elderly (pp. 195-219). Edited by Barbara Rieman Herzog. Special Publication #4, Gerontological Society. London: Human Resources Press, 1978.

Kirk, Jerome and Marc L. Miller. Reliability and Validity in Qualitative Research. Beverly Hills, California: Sage Publications, 1986.

Kolodrubetz, Walter W. "Two Decades of Employee Benefit Plans 1950-1970: A Review." Social Security Bulletin 35, no. 4 (April 1972): 10.

Korczyk, Sophie. _Retirement Security and Tax Policy_. Employee
  Benefit Research Institute, 1984.

Koski, Richard and Deborah Schneider. "The Impact of DEFRA and REA on
  U.S. Qualified Employee Benefit Plans." _Benefits International_
  (UK) 14, no. 9 (March 1985): 24-28.

Kotlikoff, Lawrence J. and Daniel E. Smith. _Pensions in the American
  Economy_. Chicago: University of Chicago Press, 1983.

Levitan, Sara A. and Martha R. Cooper. _Business Lobbies: The Public
  Good and the Bottom Line_. Baltimore: Johns Hopkins University
  Press, 1984.

Lincoln, Yvonna S. _Organizational Theory and Inquiry: The Paradigm
  Revolution_. Beverly Hills: Sage Publications, Inc., 1985.

Louis, Karen Seashore. "Multisite/Multimethod Studies." _American
  Behavioral Scientist_ 26, no. 1 (September/October 1982): 6-22.

Ludwig, Ronald L. and John E. Curtis. "ESOPs Made Substantially More
  Attractive as a Result of Economic Recovery Act." _Journal of
  Taxation_ 55 (October 1981): 208-211.

Marshall, T. H. _Class, Citizenship and Social Development_. New York:
  Doubleday, 1965.

McGill, Dan M. _Fundamentals of Private Pensions_. 5th edition.
  Homewood, Illinois: Richard D. Irwin, Inc., 1984.

Mercer, William M. _Mercer Bulletin_ 3 (September 1984). Published
  monthly by Meidinger, Incorporated.

Miller, S. M. "Reformulating the Welfare State." _Social Policy_ 15,
  no. 3 (Winter 1985): 62-64.

Munnell, Alicia H. "Social Security in a Changing Environment." In
  Aging and Income. Edited by Barbara Reiman Herzog. London:
  Human Resources Press, 1978.

_____. _The Economics of Private Pensions_. Washington, D.C.:
  Brookings Institute, 1982.

Nelson, G. H. "Tax Expenditures for the Elderly." _Gerontologist_ 23
  (October 1983): 471-478.

Ozawa, Martha N. "Work and Social Policy." In _Work, Workers and Work
  Organizations_. Edited by Sheila H. Akabar and Paul Kurzman.
  Englewood Cliffs, New Jersey: Prentice Hall, 1982.

Patton, Michael Quinn. Qualitative Evaluation Methods. Beverly
Hills, California: Sage Publications, 1980.

_____. Utilization Focused Evaluation. Beverly Hills, California:
Sage Publications, 1978.

Pine, Sidney R. and Bruce P. Wright. "Scrutinizing the Economic
Recovery Tax Act of 1981." Risk Management 29, no. 2 (February
1982): 12-19.

Rappaport, Anna M. "Update on Postretirement Medical Benefits--Issue
of the 1980s." Journal of Pension Planning and Compliance 11,
no. 4 (Winter 1985): 309-314.

Reich, Robert. Tales of a New America. New York: Times Books, 1987.

Reid, William Jr. and Audrey D. Smith. Research in Social Work.
New York: Columbia University Press, 1981.

Rein, Martin. "Equality and Social Policy." Social Service Review
51, no. 4 (December 1977): 565-587.

Root, Lawrence. Social Insurance in the Steel Industry. Beverly
Hills, California: Sage Publications, 1982.

Schultz, James H. and Thomas D. Leavitt. Pension Integration:
Concepts, Issues and Proposals. Washington, D.C.: Employee
Benefit Research Institute, 1983.

Schwarz, J. America's Hidden Survey: A Reassessment of Twenty Years
of Public Policy. New York: W. W. Norton & Co., 1983.

Shidler, Alan B. and Dawn G. Cziok. "The 1981 Economy Recovery Tax
Act: A Stimulus to Employee Benefits, Compensation and Personal
Savings Programs." Journal of Pension Planning and Compliance 7,
no. 4 (July 1981): 332-349.

"Social Security Programs in the United States." Social Security
Bulletin 50, no. 4 (April 1987): 7.

Spector, Scott P. "ESOPs and 401(k) Plans after DEFRA in Employee
Benefits Legislation, 1984." By Joseph R. Simone and Max J.
Schwartz. J4-3554 (pp. 85-106). Practicing Law Institute, 1984.

Sweeney, K. "VEBAs: Tax Planning for Universal Benefits." Financial
Executive 52, no. 9 (September 1984): 31-33.

Titmuss, Richard M. "The Irresponsible Society." In Essays on the Welfare State (pp. 215-243). By Richard M. Titmuss. London: Unwin University Books, 1963.

_____. "Pension Systems and Population Change." In Essays on the Welfare State (pp. 56-74). By Richard M. Titmuss. 2nd addition. London: George Allen and Unwin, Ltd., 1963.

_____. "The Social Division of Welfare." In Essays on the Welfare State. By Richard M. Titmuss. 2nd addition. London: George Allen and Unwin, Ltd., 1963.

_____. Commitment to Welfare. New York: Pantheon Books, 1968.

_____. "The Role of Redistribution in Social Policy." In Commitment to Welfare (pp. 188-199). By Richard M. Titmuss. London: Unwin University Books, 1968.

_____. The Gift Relationship. London: Allen & Unwin, 1971.

_____. "Welfare 'Rights', Law and Discretion." Political Quarterly 42 (1971): 113-132.

_____. Social Policy. Edited by Brian Abel-Smith and Kay Titmuss. New York: Pantheon Books, 1974.

_____. "Values and Choices." In Social Policy (pp. 132-141). By Richard Titmuss. New York: Pantheon Books, 1974.

Tullock, Gordon. Welfare for the Well-to-Do. Dallas: The Fisher Institute, 1983.

Tussing, Dale A. "The Dual Welfare System." Society 11, no. 2 (January/February 1974): 145-152.

Underwood, Don. "Toward Self-Reliance in Retirement Planning." Harvard Business Review 3 (May-June 1984).

U.S. Congress, House, Committee for Economic Development. Reforming Retirement Policies. A Statement by the Research and Policy Committee of the Committee for Economic Development, 1981.

U.S. Congress, House, Select Committee on Aging. The Future of Retirement Programs in America. Washington, D.C., Thursday, 26 February 1981.

_____. "Tenth Anniversary of the Employee Retirement Income Security Act of 1974." A Report on the Conference Proceedings, Septemeber 11, 1984. April 1985.

280

_____. "Private Pension Plans: Which Way Are They Headed?"
Committee Publication No. 99-507. Washington, D.C.: Research
Service of the Library of Congress, August 1985.

U.S. Department of Commerce, Bureau of the Census. Statistical
Abstracts of the United States. Washington, D.C.: United
States Government Printing Offices, 1985.

U.S. Department of Labor, Bureau of Labor Statistics. Employee
Benefits in Medium and Large Firms, Bulletin 2281. June 1987.

Van Maanen, J., J. M. Dabbs Jr. and Robert R. Faulkner. Varieties of
Qualitative Research. Beverly Hills, California: Sage
Publications, 1982.

Vogel, David. "The Power of Business in America: A Re-Appraisal of
Business-Government Relations and the 'Privilege Position'
Occupied by Business Corporations in the Political System."
British Journal of Political Science 13 (January 1983): 19-43.

Webb, Eugene, J. R. Campbell, D. Schwartz and Lee Schreat.
Unobtrusive Measures, Non-Reactive Research in the Social
Sciences. Chicago: Rand McNally, 1966.

Weiss, Carol H. "Bucuvalas Truth Test and Utility Test; Decision
Makers Frames of Reference for Social Science Research."
American Sociological Review (April 1980): 302-312.

Wilding, Paul. "Richard Titmuss and Social Welfare." Social and
Economic Administration 10, no. 3 (Autumn 1976): 147-166.

Wilensky, H. J. and C. N. Lebeaux, Industrial Society and Social
Welfare. New York: Free Press, 1965.

Winger, Ruth Y. The Impact of Tax Incentives on the Corporate Income
Security Planning. Coloquium Presentation to the Social Work
Faculty and Students. University of Minnesota, 12 February 1987.

Yin, Robert K. Case Study Research: Design and Method. Beverly Hills:
Sage Publications, 1984.

GLOSSARY OF DEFERRED
COMPENSATION TERMINOLOGY

actuarial equivalent: If the present values of two series of payments are equal, taking into accounting a given interest rate and mortality according to a given table, the two series are said to be actuarially equivalent on this basis. For example, a lifetime monthly benefit of $67.60 beginning at age sixty (on a given set of actuarial assumptions) can be said to be the actuarial equivalent of $100 a month beginning at age sixty-five. The actual benefit amounts are different but the present value of the two benefits, considering mortality and interest, is the same.

actuary: A person professionally trained in the technical aspects of pensions, insurance and related fields. The actuary estimates how much money must be contributed to a pension fund in order to provide future benefits.

amortization: Paying an interest-bearing liability by gradual reduction through a series of installments, as opposed to one lump-sum payment.

annuitant: A person entitled to receive payments under an annuity or now receiving such payments.

annuity: A contract that provides an income for a specified period of time, such as a number of years or for life. Annuity payments are usually made monthly but can be made quarterly, semi-annually or annually. Often used synonymously with pension.

assumptions: Conditions and rules underlying the calculation of a pension benefit, including expected interest, mortality and turnover.

beneficiary: Person named by the participant in a pension or welfare plan to receive any benefits provided by the plan if the participant dies.

break in service: A calendar year, plan year or other consecutive twelve-month period designated by the plan during which a plan participant does not complete more than 500 hours of service.

covered: A person covered by a pension plan is one who has fulfilled the eligibility requirements in the plan, for whom benefits have accrued, or are accruing, or who is receiving benefits under the plan.

death benefit: A payment made to a designated beneficiary upon the death of the employee annuitant.

deferred annuity: An annuity under which payment will begin at some definite future date, such as in a specified number of years or at a specified age.

deferred compensation: Arrangements by which compensation to employees for past or current services is postponed until some future date.

defined contribution plan: A plan under which the contribution rate is fixed and benefits to be received by employees after retirement depend to some extent upon the contributions and their earnings.

early retirement: Retirement of a participant prior to the normal retirement date, usually with a reduced amount of annuity. Early retirement is generally allowed at any time during a period of five to ten years preceding the normal retirement date.

eligibility requirements: This term refers to (a) the conditions which an employee must satisfy to participate in a retirement plan, one such condition being the completion of from one to three years of service with the employer, another the attainment of a specified age or (b) conditions which an employee must satisfy to obtain a retirement benefit, such as the completion of fifteen years of service and the attainment of age sixty-five.

Employee Stock Ownership Plan (ESOP): A defined contribution pension plan which is designated to invest primarily in employer securities.

fiduciary: One who exercises discretionary authority or control over management of a plan or disposition of its assets, renders investment advice for a fee, or has authority or responsibility to do so, or has discretionary authority or responsibility in administering a plan.

401(k) Plan: A salary reduction plan that allows employees to contribute a portion of their salaries on a tax-deferred basis.

Individual Retirement Account (IRA): An account to which an individual can make a tax-deductible annual contribution of 100% of earnings up to $2,000 ($2,250 for a one-income married couple).

integration: A coordination of the pension benefit with the Social Security benefit through a specific formula. Qualified plans must integrate so that total benefits are non-discriminatory between rank and file employees and owners, officers or highly compensated employees.

lump-sum distribution: Payment within one taxable year of the entire balance payable to an employee from a trust which forms part of a qualified pension or employee annuity plan on account of that person's death, separation from service or attainment of age 59½.

Pension Benefit Guaranty Corporation (PBGC): The federal body responsible for administering the plan termination insurance program under ERISA.

pension benefits: A series of payments to be provided in accordance with the plan of benefits.

pension plan: A plan established and maintained by an employer, group of employers, union or any combination, primarily to provide for the payment of definitely determinable benefits to participants after retirement.

plan administrator: The person or persons controlling the money or property contributed to the plan, usually designed in the plan agreement.

portability: The transfer of pension rights and credits when a worker changes jobs.

qualified plan: A plan which the Internal Revenue Service approves as meeting the requirements of Section 401(a) of the 1954 Internal Revenue code. Such plans receive tax advantages.

self-administered (trusteed or directly invested) plan: A plan funded through a fiduciary, generally a bank, but sometimes a group of individuals, which directly invests the accumulated funds. Retirement payments are made from the fund as they fall due.

spouse's benefit: Payments to the surviving spouse of a deceased employee, usually in the form of a series of payments upon meeting certain requirements and usually terminating with the survivor's remarriage or death.

transferability: Any arrangement under which the accumulated benefit credits of a terminating participant, or their actuarial value, are transmitted from one plan to another, or to a central agency.

turnover rate: The rate at which employees terminate covered service other than by death or retirement. Expected future turnover can be taken into account in translating contributions into benefits.

vesting: A provision that a pension participant will, after meeting certain requirements, retain a right to all or part of the accrued benefits, even though the employee may leave the job before retirement.

For Product Safety Concerns and Information please contact our EU representative GPSR@taylorandfrancis.com
Taylor & Francis Verlag GmbH, Kaufingerstraße 24, 80331 München, Germany